Praise for
God's Mercy Awaits You

"In *God's Mercy Awaits You*, you will find wise and compassionate assistance in helping to heal an abortion loss. This book is also helpful to those who love someone who has had an abortion and is in need of healing, by helping them to understand the issues and providing resources."

—Vicki Thorn, foundress of Project Rachel
and executive director of the National Office of
Post-Abortion Reconciliation and Healing

"Many people associated with the Catholic Church, and with churches that are strongly evangelical in nature, are noted for their strongly pro-life stance. We should never forget, however, that the Church in its core structure is also strongly pro-healing and pro-mercy, reflecting the divine mercy of Jesus from the cross.

"Sister Patricia Marie Barnette beautifully portrays how that healing and mercy are at work for those seeking the Lord's healing and peace. 'Each day God continues to heal you' is the wonderful message you will take from this insightful and uplifting book."

—Most Reverend Robert J. Baker, S.T.D., Bishop of Birmingham, Alabama

"Many women live for years in isolation with the pain of a past abortion. *God's Mercy Awaits You* is both the title and the message of a unique book by Sr. Patricia Marie Barnette, which draws on her extensive experience in post-abortion healing ministry. *God's Mercy Awaits You* offers hope and practical encouragement to all those suffering from post-abortion pain. It also provides invaluable insights to friends, family members, and those involved in the Church's Project Rachel ministry."

—Marianne Luthin, Director, Pro-Life Office and Project Rachel, Archdiocese of Boston

"*God's Mercy Awaits You* by Sr. Patricia Marie Barnette is a powerful gift to women who have had abortions and to their family members. Barnette combines the experiences of numerous women with spiritual truths and empirical research on the psychological implications of abortion to lead women to a place of mercy and peace. Many women experience religious conversions in the aftermath of an abortion or deepen their personal relationships with God, yet struggle with forgiving themselves. This amazing book provides deep compassionate understanding of the challenges women face after abortion, and offers gentle substantive guidance on the path to complete healing and renewed hope."

—Priscilla K. Coleman, Ph.D., professor of Human Development and Family Studies, Bowling Green State University, Bowling Green, Ohio

"Abortion can leave those who experience it with the belief that they have committed an unforgiveable sin, with no hope of peace and salvation. But God is Mercy himself and longs to heal us if we seek him out in sorrow.

"For almost three decades now, I have been working in the Entering Canaan Ministry, which is based on my own journey of healing with God. Originally developed with the Sisters of Life for women, it has since expanded with the help of the Franciscan Friars of the Renewal to include retreats for men, siblings, and those who abort due to an adverse diagnosis. We have been blessed to see God at work in the lives of thousands of people as they come to know his love and mercy and learn the dynamics of healing.

"In *God's Mercy Awaits You*, a book on abortion healing written by Patricia Marie Barnette, RGS, she shares her personal knowledge and experience of working with those seeking healing with a beautiful invitation into his heart through scripture passages, as well as practical psychological insights to help address the many psychological dynamics encountered on the healing journey.

"Although we are not our abortions, their impact is deep. However, through the loving mercy of God we are shown our dignity as his children and led to the fountain of his mercy where hope abides.

"God is waiting for you! Seek him out in the pages of this book and you will find he has always been there."

—Theresa Bonopartis, Director, Lumina/Hope and Healing
after Abortion; Co-Developer, Entering Canaan—
A Sacramental Journey to an Inheritance of Mercy

God's Mercy
Awaits You

God's Mercy Awaits You

Find Healing after Abortion

By Patricia Marie Barnette, RGS

Pauline
BOOKS & MEDIA
Boston

Library of Congress Control Number: 2019952896
CIP data is available.

ISBN-10: 0-8198-3159-X
ISBN-13: 978-0-8198-3159-0

Cover design by Rosanna Usselmann

Cover photo: istockphoto.com/© StudioM1

Published by Pauline Books & Media, 50 Saint Pauls Avenue, Boston, MA 02130-3491

Printed in the U.S.A.

www.pauline.org

Pauline Books & Media is the publishing house of the Daughters of St. Paul, an international congregation of women religious serving the Church with the communications media.

1 2 3 4 5 6 7 8 9   24 23 22 21 20

Contents

*This book is dedicated to Our Lady of Guadalupe
and to all the courageous women who have opened
their hearts to walk the healing journey
from darkness to the light of Christ.*

Foreword

"In hope we were saved," (Rom 8:24).

The cry from the heart of a woman who has suffered an abortion is, in our experience as Sisters of Life, invariably, "Is there hope for me?" It is an almost universal and often hesitant question. The one suffering holds her breath in fear, waiting for the answer. The answer comes in an instant, pouring out of the Father's merciful and tender heart: "Do not fear, for I have redeemed you . . . you are precious in my eyes, and honored, and I love you," (Is 43:1, 4). Is there hope? There is so much hope—for you, and for us all!

Through our Hope and Healing Mission, we Sisters of Life accompany hundreds of women each year along the path of hope toward healing from their abortion experiences. What a great privilege it is to be invited into the darkest places of another's heart, and to see the Light of

Christ dispel her deepest fear: that she is alone in her suffering. We have witnessed time and again that transformation occurs when a woman trusts enough to reach out for the hand of another and comes to know she is not only not alone, but loved in her sinfulness and suffering. What a stunning truth—this mysterious, glorious, unfathomable mercy of God!

In *God's Mercy Awaits You*, Sister Patricia offers an introduction to this process and points us to Christ's infinite mercy and love. She shares stories of women and men, whom she has accompanied over the years, who have found hope and healing after their abortions. She also explores different facets of the healing process itself. Sister uses Scripture so beautifully to illustrate and ground her words in the Truth that sets us free. And so, whether you have suffered the effects of abortion yourself or are supporting another seeking healing, this book may be a source of comfort and encouragement.

Each person's journey is unique, and Jesus has a particular plan for *your* healing. Navigating with you through the pain, suffering, and grief that follow an abortion, and restoring you to a place of peace and calm, is his great desire. As Sister Patricia mentions, our identity does not lie in the choices we make or in the sins we commit, but in the fact that we are created in the image and likeness of God. We are his beloved.

Many women find it helpful to attend a retreat, join a support group, or meet regularly with a priest, counselor, or other trusted advisor. *God's Mercy Awaits You* is an aid both for those who have suffered an abortion, as well as for the friends, relatives, professionals, and others who minister to them.

My sincere prayer for you is that you will find within these pages a helpful resource—one of encouragement and guidance—as you embark on this journey, and that the Lord will grant you the grace of perseverance in seeking healing, peace, and wholeness. Everything is possible with God!

May God richly bless you, and may Christ, the Lord of Life, heal all that is broken and restore you to newness of life.

"Behold, I make all things new," (Rev 21:5).

"I came so that they might have life and have it more abundantly," (Jn 10:10).

MOTHER AGNES MARY DONOVAN, SV
Superior General, Sisters of Life

Is This Book for You?

Love is calling you.

If you have ever had an abortion, and you find it difficult to resolve its effects, reading this book and praying over the Scriptures can help you find the tranquility and wholeness you have been searching for. Jesus is calling you to receive and live his peace, which is beyond any peace that this world gives. Jesus is the healer of all hurts. This book is an invitation to receive this healing.

Did your inner life change after the abortion? Do you feel as if your life has not moved forward since that day? Do shame and low self-esteem keep you at an emotional distance from other people? Do you have trouble sleeping or have nightmares about your baby? Is it difficult for you to concentrate on studies, work, or other tasks? Do you get anxious around the anniversary date of the abortion or near the date your child would have been born? Does being around pregnant women or babies make you uncomfortable? Do you lack interest in joyful life events? Did you turn to alcohol or drug abuse after the abortion to deaden inner pain?

Do you have an undying hope that your life can turn around, in spite of all this? That you can find peace and happiness again, even though you may feel you have lost a part of yourself?

This book can be a part of your journey to be restored to the fullness of life that Jesus promises all of us. His mercy and love await you. Do not be afraid to come to *life*.

If you are a family member or friend seeking ways to help someone you love, or if you are a counselor or pastoral minister, this book can help you too. It can guide you to help others who may disclose a past abortion and share all the difficulties that have occurred in its aftermath.

Introduction

Jesus is waiting to heal you. Healing! We all seek healing from the hurts of life. If you have had one or more abortions in the past, and you now have trouble putting all the pieces together so you can live your life in peace, I hope that you will find comfort, tranquility, and courage in the pages of this book.

Abortion can have many negative effects on a person's life, including depression, anxiety, addiction, and other psychological and physical symptoms of trauma. This book invites you to allow yourself to grieve—over the loss of your precious child, over the loss of innocence and dreams, over fragmented relationships. Blocked grief buries pain, anger, and sorrow deep inside and prevents healing and freedom.

Our society tends to look the other way regarding the negative effects of abortion. Some people deny any ill effects whatsoever. As a result, a woman or man affected by abortion may not feel free to mourn the loss of a child due to the abortion. Often abortion is a deeply kept secret. I hope that you will give yourself permission to acknowledge your sorrow, to mourn, and to heal.

Although this book focuses mainly on healing for women, it devotes one chapter to the unique way in which men grieve the loss of a child due to abortion. Most who come for healing are women. Unfortunately, too many men suffer silently about their participation in the abortion decision. Family members also mourn the loss of a grandchild, niece or nephew, brother or sister. Appendix 3 lists resources to help women, men, and family members who are searching for healing.

Suggested Scripture passages are listed at the end of each chapter. They may be helpful for you to ponder and to listen to God speaking to your heart. You may discover other passages that are more helpful to you. Please see the Appendix 1 and 2 for tips on how to look up and pray with Scripture passages. At the end of each chapter you will also find reflection questions for yourself, along with tips for family members and friends.

This book is only an introduction to the process of grieving and healing. Words can be inadequate to describe the experiences and realities of loss and healing. That said, this book shares what I have learned from the many women, men, and family members who have shared their stories with me over my years as a counselor, as well as in informal settings. Each story is unique, as is each person's journey to freedom. Yet we find common elements in the very human experience of loss, grief, isolation, buried emotions, floods of tears, and the desire to be whole. Courage has brought many people to a place of calm, inner reconciliation, and a strengthening of the entire person—body, mind, and spirit—with the grace of God.

I have also been educated through psychological studies, workshops, and friends and colleagues who work in this ministry. For me, this journey has been a call within a call. Having been very active in various aspects of pro-life work leading up to Project Rachel's founding in the mid 1980s, I felt a deep calling to get involved in helping others to heal from the severe wound of abortion. I am a Sister of the Good Shepherd, a religious order whose charism involves living out the belief that "a person is of more value than a world" (in the words of Saint Mary Euphrasia, our founder). This vision urges me to reach out to those who are most in need of God's mercy, those who are most brokenhearted. This call led me to get a master's degree in counseling psychology, with subsequent licensure as a professional clinical counselor in two states. I have volunteered in several dioceses with Project Rachel and have assisted in a peer ministry for more than twenty years. I have also counseled people through various agencies and healing ministries. The integration of psychology and spirituality used throughout this book offers a broader approach to healing.

It's my deep desire that women, men, and families experience renewal of healthy relationships by being healed after an abortion. As the prophet Jeremiah says: "Then it is as if fire is burning in my heart, / imprisoned in my bones; / I grow weary holding back" (Jer 20:9). Jesus Christ is the healer, and he invites others to be his instruments in this process.

To Jesus Christ be the glory. Entrust to him your desire for healing, and you will find yourself made new in the ocean of his mercy and love. God has his own time and way of leading each person along the road to the fullness he envisions for you.

Let yourself be found by the Lord, healed and forgiven, just like this client I accompanied on the healing process:

❦❧❦❧❦

Carina was able to say with such honesty when her life was restored: "My life changed so drastically after the abortion, that I did not recognize myself.

For years I isolated myself from those people I loved and drowned my pain in the numbness of alcohol. When I couldn't take the darkness anymore, I reached out to God for help. I never thought my life could be filled with so much peace after God gave me the courage to seek help and to be free of this suffering. With the help of counseling and prayer, I came to understand why I made this decision and found that facing the truth enabled me to forgive and to accept forgiveness."[1]

---

1. Client stories are either used with permission of the persons involved or are composites in which names and identifying details have been changed to protect the privacy of individuals.

The Broken Vessel

When we shatter and break into pieces,
    like a dry earthen vessel,
We sometimes activate tears from the well
    of our soul.
These tears have been buried so deep that it is
painful for them to travel the long journey
    to the surface.
They emerge carrying the pain which has been
lying hidden for so many years.
This process can be:
So painful yet so freeing
So frightening yet so encouraging
So depleting yet so refreshing.

These tears initially are rusty.
They are full of the hurts and disappointments
    of our life.
As they flow the tears become more pure and clear,
Like a beautiful stream in the summertime.

The tears moisten the dry, broken pieces.
The Potter carefully gathers all the little fragments
    and begins to work them in his hands.

He forms them back into the vessel's original
    design.
He restores the vessel and makes it new.
This time it has been strengthened through the
    tears and through his hands.
The new vessel is restored.
It is now capable of holding clean, fresh water
    to provide refreshment for others.

*Written by a woman
who has been on the journey*

CHAPTER 1

Encouragement for the Journey

Merciful and gracious is the LORD,
   slow to anger, abounding in mercy. . . .
But the LORD's mercy is from age to age,
toward those who fear him.

Psalm 103:8, 17

The Lord hears the cry of the poor. The Lord God hears *your* cry. *Your* cry for healing. *Your* cry to be free of the pain, the isolation, the grief, the guilt. *Your* cry for a new life. God loves *you*. If you are suffering from a previous abortion or abortions, God will give you the courage you need to find peace. Jesus desires to heal you. Yes, *you!* You deeply desire to be as you were before the pain and suffering entered your life. Jesus will restore you and give you new life.

The cry from within your heart may shout, "No, I don't deserve it, I can never be forgiven!"

Now is the time to listen to the voice of the Good Shepherd, who desires to lead you into the pastures of hope, the land of sunshine and fresh breezes, waters that take away the dryness of the desert. No one is beyond the reach of the mercy of God! You are not beyond the reach of God's mercy. God is love. God is mercy. You are his child. Mercy is for *you*. Healing is for *you*. Forgiveness is for *you*. There is no sin that God will not forgive. New life is for *you*. Come to the waters of peace and restoration.

Words of Encouragement

Take time to ponder these words of women who have been through the healing journey to recovery. They share these words with you to encourage you to take that first step, or to continue, if you have begun. These women have great love and hope for your healing. One of them says:

> No matter what thoughts came into my mind, it all was okay because God was with me. . . . I could look back into my past and place it all with the Lord. Praise Jesus! I could see my past with different eyes and knew it would be okay! I was no longer looking back into my past alone; I was looking back with God.

Another woman recounts:

> For too long I tried to create my own serenity by using substances to numb the pain; by agreeing with others, even if I didn't, just to avoid conflicts; and by minimizing the hurts others have caused me. I then recognized that all these efforts for serenity were actually causing me anxiety. Peace was not to be found within my broken heart. Peace would only be found in the broken heart of Christ.

The Lord will send people to help you on this journey. You may fear that once a person hears your story, that person may reject you. Trust takes time to build. If you feel safe with a person, that is a good sign. Testing the waters by taking small steps can help you feel secure enough to take a bigger risk in sharing next time. When you find a person who will listen with compassion to your story, your sorrows, your hopes and dreams, do not be afraid. If the listener stays with you, now you have found a person who is willing to share in your difficulties and accompany you to hope and healing.

It is important to be careful about sharing your story. You have no obligation to go public with your story. Your integrity as a person, the needs of your family, and your mental health must be protected. Careful discernment in deciding whom to tell and when to tell is important as you continue to journey to health. You will find more about relationships in Chapter 7, but for now know this: Priests, ministers, religious sisters, peer companions, Project Rachel volunteers, and Christian counselors are trained to help you through the difficult phases. Appendix 3 in this book lists online resources for locating licensed Catholic therapists located near you.

For many years, I have been entrusted with the stories of women who express pain and sorrow over the decision to abort a child. It is difficult to accept the death of a child, especially one in the womb, especially a child who dies through abortion. Many women say that a part of them died, or went dormant, when their child died. In some sense, their emotional life became stuck in time, at the moment of the death of their child. Perhaps you, like many women, have gone into emotional isolation. You appear healthy on the outside, but you suffer deeply on the inside. Other relationships may be ruptured, such as with the father of the child, with your husband, with other children, with other family members, and with friends. Often self-respect and self-worth plummet, while shame and self-criticism take over.

Many women have suffered in silence for a long time—some for decades, some for a lifetime. Women are often afraid to seek help. Perhaps you fear that everyone will find out about the abortion and you will be rejected. Or perhaps you are anxious that the process will be too painful. But now you have so many opportunities to seek and find joy, peace, and newness of life. When you decide to begin the steps toward healing, your outlook will begin to improve as hope emerges. Facing the pain that already exists helps resolve the issues and integrate the solutions into your life. Your pain will lessen as peace, understanding, and acceptance gain a greater part in your life.

You may fear that if you go through the healing process, you will forget the child you have lost. Be at peace and know that this will not happen. The wonderful process that does happen is that you begin to accept yourself as a person of worth and dignity, to accept your role as mother of this child who now lives in the presence of God, and to connect with your child on a spiritual level. Letting go of pain, anger, guilt, and bitterness opens the door to living in peace. God will send gentle rain to soothe your soul, and waterfalls of grace to refresh you.

You may fear that abortion is the unforgiveable sin. But if you are truly sorry, no sin is unforgiveable. Jesus died on the Cross to free every single person who has ever lived or ever will live.

Mercy is for you too.

This woman made the decision to trust God on his word:

❖⤛❖⤜❖

Laurel sat very still, holding a small crucifix in her hands. For several months she had made progress in healing, as she faithfully attended our weekly therapy session and explored the reasons and events that led to her decision to abort her first child. At the age of fifteen, she had become pregnant. For a year she had been going with an older crowd of friends who introduced her to drinking, drugs, and sex. She was rebelling against the chaos of her family life. When her mother found out Laurel was pregnant, she told her to either get an abortion or get out of the house. Laurel felt she had to comply, as she didn't want to be out on the street. However, she did not want to have an abortion. Immediately afterward, she had difficulty trusting anyone and became very depressed.

Fifteen years later, as she matured, Laurel knew she needed help to deal with her past actions. She had a very difficult time forgiving herself. Laurel seemed to not be able to move forward. She was stuck. So one day, I suggested that she hold a small crucifix in her hands. I asked her to gaze on Jesus, who loves her so much, and to believe in his promise of mercy and forgiveness. While she gazed in silence, I prayed silently for her. After some time, Laurel starting weeping. The impasse was broken by the saving grace of Jesus flowing into her heart. Laurel was able to pardon herself and began to live a life of joy, immersed in the love and mercy of Jesus.

❧☙❧☙❧

Believe in Jesus' words from the Cross: "Father, forgive them, they know not what they do" (Lk 23:34). Those words of truth will set you free. Jesus' love and mercy are so immense that he would give his life to save even one person. Each person is of infinite worth to our merciful God.

Women have abortions when they are single, divorced, or married; rich, poor, or with moderate income; during the early years of fertility, and near the end of the fertile years—in other words, women have abortions in many situations. Since 1973, when statistics began to be kept, millions of women in the United States have had at least one abortion.[1] This means that we are all affected by the

---

1. For real-time statistics on the numbers of abortions in the United States and worldwide, see the abortion counters at "Number of Abortions - Abortion Counters," http://www.numberofabortions.com.

fallout of abortion. Few families do not have a member who has suffered from an abortion, whether it is general knowledge or not. The negative effects of abortion touch the entire family.

That is why the restoration of one woman also heals others in her family. It heals her friendships. Healing can break patterns of generational dysfunction. The healing of one woman can prevent another abortion. The healing of families helps to heal a nation. And our nation needs much recovery of health and wholeness regarding the sanctity of human life.

The Healing Process

We will cover the specifics of the healing process in greater depth throughout this book. In brief, most women go through several main phases of healing to integrate and understand this event in their lives. However, it is important to understand that each journey is as unique as the individual woman. Your journey may be similar to others' journeys in some areas and may be very different in other aspects. Please do not compare your progress to that of another person. God knows exactly what *you* need so that you may experience his love and understanding. You may need to look at issues that caused difficulties in your life before you were pregnant. You may be facing difficult issues in your life right now. The abortion did not happen in isolation from the other aspects of your life at that time. Examining whatever prevents your progress is so important to becoming a whole person. As you open yourself to God's grace, your true beauty will unfold, and you will be washed with the joy and mercy of the infinite love of God.

Healing takes time. It is important not to become overwhelmed emotionally, so you must go at a comfortable pace. Be gentle with yourself. You may have many spiritual, emotional, and psychological layers to uncover and expose to the loving light of Christ. Find the support that you need so you do not make this journey alone. Find a person with whom you feel safe so you can open your heart. The Holy Spirit will give you all the courage and strength you need to start and continue this important work. Helpful resources are listed at the end of this book.

To begin, have hope as you reconnect with God in a personal relationship. You arc God's creation, his loving daughter. As Father Michael Mannion states in his book *Abortion & Healing*: "The author of life is he who must heal the loss of life."[2] Do not hesitate to approach the God

---

2. Michael T. Mannion, *Abortion & Healing: A Cry to Be Whole* (Kansas City: Sheed & Ward, 1986), 82.

of mercy! God knows your heart and knows more about you than you do about yourself.

Accepting God's mercy and forgiveness enables you to open spaces in your heart to begin forgiving others and forgiving yourself. Examining your anger toward each person who was involved in the abortion decision will bring you greater freedom and openness to new life for yourself. Holding on to anger binds you and can make you ill on many levels. It is like having your hands full of thorns that cut and burn. Until you drop these thorns, you cannot pick up beautiful flowers to admire. Removing your bitterness makes space for love and forgiveness of others. This freedom allows you to be involved in life—no longer just looking longingly out of a window. You can now open the door and step outside into the marvelous varieties of joy that life offers.

When this space inside your heart is open, the opportunity to explore your relationship with your child comes to you as a gift. Experiencing the personhood of this child helps you to accept your role as a mother. This precious child is your child forever. Your child loves you and forgives you. To accept this love and forgiveness opens the gateway for you to experience a spiritual relationship with your beautiful child, until you see each other face to face in Heaven.

The most difficult work is forgiveness of self. We are often harder on ourselves than we are on others. I often ask the women I work with: "What would you say to your best friend if she told you of a similar experience in her life?" The kindness you would show to a friend can also be shown to yourself. Become your own best friend. God always sees the best in you.

Be aware, also, that healing does not happen in an orderly manner. The journey has ups and downs, perhaps circling back for a deeper restoration in an area you already explored. There are no rules to follow. Your journey is guided by Jesus, the Good Shepherd, who "calls his own sheep by name and leads them out. . . . He walks ahead of them, and the sheep follow him, because they recognize his voice" (Jn 10:3, 4). Listen for the voice of the one who loves you beyond all imagining. Let the healing spring rain of Jesus' love and grace pour over your wounded soul and make you whole.

Courage! Your innermost self will release beauty and grace to radiate God's love to all who are privileged to know you.

Scripture Meditations on God's Mercy

❖   Psalm 103

❖   Ezekiel 34:15–16

❖ Matthew 11:28–30

❖ Revelation 3:20

Reflection Questions

❖ Why did you decide to read this book at this point in your life?

❖ What are you seeking?

❖ What gives you encouragement now?

❖ Remember a difficult situation in which you felt God was blessing you, and thank God for it.

❖ What are your plans for seeking support in your healing journey?

Tips for Family Members and Friends

❖ If you know someone who has had an abortion (family member, friend, co-worker), you might be concerned for her well-being. If she has not come to you for help, however, it is best to wait until she is ready to disclose her story or ask for your help. As much as you want healing for this person, it is important to respect her boundary for privacy. She may not be ready to talk. Approaching her if she is not ready may push her farther away. Instead, prayer and kindness go a long way and give

much comfort. Accepting her in love is very healing in itself.

❖ If someone you know does ask to talk, the most
important thing to do first is to listen to her and
not be frightened by what she may disclose. If she
is feeling shame, she may feel that others will think
badly of her, too. Your presence assures her that
you are willing to stay and listen—that you care
about her as an individual. You are showing God's
mercy to her.

CHAPTER 2

Aftereffects of Abortion: Trauma, Depression, Anxiety, and Addictions

You who dwell in the shelter of the Most High,
  who abide in the shade of the Almighty,
Say to the Lord, "My refuge and fortress,
  my God in whom I trust."
He will rescue you from the fowler's snare,
  from the destroying plague,
He will shelter you with his pinions,
  and under his wings you may take refuge;
  his faithfulness is a protecting shield.
You shall not fear the terror of the night
  nor the arrow that flies by day,
Nor the pestilence that roams in darkness,
  nor the plague that ravages at noon.

Psalm 91:1–6

Information is power, so this chapter is filled with information. If you feel that your life is like a shattered mirror and you are always trying to put the pieces back together, perhaps the information presented here will help you discover some of those missing parts.

What does trauma have to do with abortion? Abortion is a traumatic event, one that can leave many physical, spiritual, and psychological scars. Many women say that they felt very different immediately after the abortion and remained stuck in this state until they realized they needed healing. The information in this chapter can help you make the connection between the abortion and its traumatic aftereffects. This knowledge can then shed light on unhealthy behaviors that you may have developed to bury the pain. For example, some people turn to drugs, alcohol, or risky sexual behavior in an attempt to deaden feelings of dread resulting from the trauma. Traumatic events can alter brain chemistry and bring other physical changes that adversely affect a person's well-being. Understanding all these effects can help you unwrap the layers of trauma and sorrow. Be assured of God's help for shedding light on your painful experiences:

> The LORD is my light and my salvation;
>   whom should I fear?

The LORD is my life's refuge;
    of whom should I be afraid?
When evildoers come at me
    to devour my flesh,
These my enemies and foes
    themselves stumble and fall.
Though an army encamp against me,
    my heart does not fear;
Though war be waged against me,
    even then do I trust. (Ps 27:1–3)

According to the *Diagnostic and Statistical Manual of Mental Disorders, 5th Edition* (DSM-5)—which guides mental health professionals to understand how best to help people—trauma can trigger post-traumatic stress disorder (PTSD). Types of trauma include any serious risk of death or injury from a life-threatening or violent event, as well as witnessing such an event or hearing about what happened to a loved one. Trauma could be caused by natural events, such as severe storms or an accident. Or it could be caused by any act of violence, including military battle, sexual violence, or other violent events.[1]

---

1. See American Psychiatric Association, *Diagnostic and Statistical Manual of Mental Disorders, 5th Edition: DSM-5* (Washington, DC: American Psychiatric Publishing, 2013), 271; henceforth cited as DSM-5.

The following are the symptoms of this disorder, one or more of which need to be present for over three months to be termed PTSD:

- ❖ Unwanted and uncontrollable memories of the traumatic event;

- ❖ Recurrent nightmares and sleep disturbances;

- ❖ Flashbacks as if the trauma were occurring in the present;

- ❖ Triggers of the trauma that may cause great distress, such as sounds, smells, places, persons, and events that lead to avoidance;

- ❖ Shifts in thought and mood, such as lack of memories about the event, negative thoughts of self-worth, a feeling that the world is dangerous;

- ❖ Distorted thinking;

- ❖ Negative emotions that can overwhelm a person, such as fear, shame, and horror;

- ❖ Exaggerated startle response, such as jumping at the slightest noise;

- ❖ Hypervigilance, such as always being afraid something terrible will occur;

- ❖ Lack of concentration;

◈ Increase in anger and aggression without cause;

◈ Reckless behavior.

Socially a person may experience emotional detachment and isolation from others, including those to whom one is close, and a lack of interest in daily events. It may be difficult to experience any positive emotions, and this lack can lead to significant impairment in relationships, work, education, and other social areas of life.[2] Consider the story of Rhondel:

◈⌇◈⌇◈

Rhondel had a history of major neglect and abuse as a child in her family of origin. She came from a large family in a farming area. As an adult, she had a successful professional career, yet she lacked self-esteem. She sought help for depression and anxiety from other counselors and medical professionals yet found no relief. She came to see me for healing from an abortion she'd had many years prior. The abortion was another trauma on top of childhood abuse and neglect she had never resolved. For years, Rhondel

---

2. See *DSM-5*, 271–2.

had nightmares about babies in distress. Her first-trimester abortion was done without anesthesia. She had flashbacks when she heard certain noises from machines. She never had any other children. Through some time of struggle, Rhondel was able to reestablish her relationship with God and find peace through accepting his forgiveness. She was finally able to sleep through the night without nightmares. The flashbacks stopped. Healing and peace helped to restore her to the new life that Jesus faithfully gave her as she sought his love.

❖⤙⤙❖⤚⤚❖

Many triggers or cues may cause psychological distress for someone who has had an abortion—triggers such as seeing a pregnant woman, or being near the hospital or facility where the abortion took place. Women report that such distress leads them to avoid being near babies or young children, avoid going to baby showers, and skip the baby section at stores. Women in counseling also report they are unable to remember the date of the abortion, or the name of the abortion facility. One young woman had an abortion because she wanted to finish her education—but she was so upset after the abortion and unable to focus on her studies that she dropped out of school. Stories like these are very sad, because no one warns women about possible negative effects after abortion.

But God knows each sorrow, fear, and difficulty, and he desires to help you.

How many are my foes, LORD!
  How many rise against me! . . .
But you, LORD, are a shield around me;
  my glory, you keep my head high.
With my own voice I will call out to the LORD,
  and he will answer me from his holy
      mountain. . . .
Salvation is from the LORD!
  May your blessing be upon your people!
      (Ps 3:2, 4–5, 9)

Ongoing research is being conducted on the negative effects of abortion on women. One of the leading researchers, Priscilla Coleman, has found that the risk of mental health problems in general can increase up to 81 percent following an abortion. Another aftereffect is an increased risk of alcohol addiction, at 110 percent higher than the general population. And when someone is using drugs or alcohol, she can't begin to unpack the trauma. The addiction issues need to be dealt with first, and then the healing process from the root trauma can begin.

Meanwhile, the risk for suicidal behaviors is very high, 155 percent higher than the risk in the general population.[3] If you are having suicidal thoughts or plans, please call the National Suicide Prevention Lifeline (800-273-8255) or call 911 for immediate help.

Depression is also a major difficulty. Women who have had an abortion have a 37 percent increased risk of developing depression.[4] Isolation from people with whom you used to be close can lead you to feel detached from others, which may lead to a lack of interest in family events or celebrations. Feelings of lowered self-esteem, shame, and distrust of others can come flooding into your entire sense of self. Many women report not being able to control anger at others and self. The following situation highlights the isolation that can follow an abortion.

---

3. For more about the effects of abortion on mental health, including substance abuse, see "Overview of Meta-Analysis on Abortion and Mental Health Published in British Journal of Psychiatry," WeCare (World Expert Consortium for Abortion Research and Education), accessed June 30, 2019, https://wecareexperts.org/sites/default/files/articles/Overview%20 of%20meta-analysis%20on%20abortion%20and%20mental%20 health%20published%20in%20British%20Journal%20of%20Psychiatry. pdf; see original article at P. K. Coleman, "Abortion and Mental Health: A Quantitative Synthesis and Analysis of Research Published from 1995-2009," British Journal of Psychiatry 199, no. 3 (September 2011): 180–186.

4. See "Meta-Analysis on Abortion."

❖⌖❖⌖❖

Jane had a chemical abortion at home, after receiving pills from her doctor. She was a single woman in her early forties who had been in a long-time affair with John, a married man. Jane kept hoping against all odds that this man would leave his wife and family for her, but it never happened. Jane maintained the status quo out of loneliness and fear. When she told John she was pregnant, he broke off the affair and refused to see her or talk to her. Now Jane felt really alone. She believed she had no one to turn to, because she lived an isolated life and was not close to family members. Besides, in whom could she confide, given that she was the "other woman"? She thought that the abortion was her only way out of this situation. To raise a child alone at her age was a thought she did not want to entertain. Jane never considered placing the baby for adoption. Having no connection with a church and no supportive community of friends, she went to her doctor. The pregnancy was still early enough that the doctor offered a chemical abortion. This seemed to her to be the answer, another way to hide from others and from herself. The doctor gave her instructions but failed to tell her of the negative side of a chemical abortion. She was all alone at home; and when the process began, she was unprepared for the intensity of the pain. She was traumatized by the entire experience. Now triggers in her own home reminded her of the trauma. Jane began to have additional fears of being alone, of taking medications, of going to the doctor, of doing anything that reminded her of this frightening experience.

❖❀❖❀❖

Psychological distress may recur each year near the date of the abortion and again around the anniversary of the date the child would have been born. The woman might not be fully aware, yet she realizes that things just don't go right around those times. The news surrounding the January 22 anniversary of the Supreme Court's decision to legalize abortion, *Roe v. Wade*, also causes much stress, as reported by many women who have talked to me. The symptoms of past trauma may keep people from protecting themselves from further harm or can lead to an inability to make clear decisions, which can cause additional difficulties.

Many women initially have some traumatic symptoms after an abortion. Anxiety can overwhelm a woman if she cannot calm her emotions; other chapters of this book deal with the negative effects of such anxiety. One-half of people who have experienced trauma will have a resolution of their symptoms within three months of the event.[5]

But around 20 percent of those in the general population who have experienced a traumatic event develop full-blown, chronic PTSD.[6] PTSD was recognized by medical professions as a psychological disorder after doctors truly listened to the distress of soldiers returning from the Vietnam War. Many women who have had abortions suffer from the same symptoms. These very serious problems can develop even years after the abortion occurred.

As a society, we must pay attention to the traumatic symptoms that affect these women. It is so important for women who suffer from mental health issues after an abortion to seek professional help. If you are seeking a Catholic professional therapist, resources are listed in Appendix 3. Be sure to see a therapist who is grounded in the Catholic Christian understanding of the human person and in the traditions of the faith.

---

5. See DSM-5, 277.

6. For more on PTSD, see PTSD Alliance, "Traumatic Stress Disorder Fact Sheet," Sidran Institute, accessed June 30, 2019, https://www.sidran.org/wp-content/uploads/2018/11/Post-Traumatic Stress Disorder Fact Sheet-.pdf.

If you have experienced the trauma of abortion, a professional should help you feel safe while exploring the issues that surrounded your abortion decision. That is the first step to healing. Building trust with the person accompanying you on the healing journey, within a safe and comfortable space, enables you to be calm. Traumatized persons can become afraid of their own normal bodily sensations and feelings, fearing to get too close to the memories of the trauma (these are called negative bodily sensations). They also miss out on normal positive sensations and feelings, which help people feel alive. Again, some try to escape these negative feelings in unhealthy ways by abusing drugs or alcohol, getting into abusive relationships, or isolating themselves.

If you feel this way, you'll need help to become aware of your bodily reactions to triggers, to learn how to cope with these reactions, and to feel joy again during positive experiences and sensations. Learning these differences and becoming comfortable with normal feelings can open your life to the joys, peace, excitement, and happiness God intends. This learning is a step to growth. Our bodies give us many clues regarding feelings of fear, joy, surprise, peace, disquiet, and so on. Learning your own clues will help you be more in control of your whole self: body, mind, and spirit. This skill leads to peace and self-knowledge.

If you have experienced any of these distressing symptoms since your abortion, be sure to work with a professional who encourages you to discuss only what you are comfortable disclosing or sharing. Forcing you to relive memories or retell traumatic events can traumatize you again.

Perhaps all this information will help you understand the "why" of unhealthy behaviors you may have developed as ways to survive. Then you can learn to cope in ways that lead to peace and health. Jesus will help you to put these shattered pieces of your life back together. He will show you your true and beautiful self in a mirror that reflects his love and care for you. Beauty, goodness, and truth are deep within your being. These will shine forth again for you.

The following chapters discuss the important aspects of finding this new life of freedom. Walk the path of restoration to discover your authentic identity as a beautiful daughter of our loving God.

Scripture Meditations on God's Protective Love

- ❖ Psalm 91
- ❖ Luke 8:26–36
- ❖ Matthew 14:22–33

Reflection Questions

◈ Have you personally experienced any of the symptoms described in this chapter? What are they, and how have they affected your life?

◈ Do you have hope that you can find peace? If not, what can you do to find this hope?

◈ Do you also need to heal from other traumas in your life, either before or after the abortion? How can you address these issues?

◈ Are you aware of messages your body sends you if you ever feel unsafe in a situation or around a particular person? How do you respond to these messages?

Tips for Family Members and Friends

◈ If your loved one suffers from an addiction, encourage her to get help. She can't heal from the abortion until she works on being substance-free.

◈ The healing process has many layers. Be patient with your loved one.

CHAPTER 3

Connecting with God

For I know well the plans I have in mind for you . . .
plans for your welfare and not for woe, so as to give you
a future of hope. When you call me, and come and pray
to me, I will listen to you. When you look for me, you
will find me. Yes, when you seek me with all your heart,
I will let you find me . . . and I will change your lot.

Jeremiah 29:11–14

After having an abortion, women often speak of feeling cut off from God. They think that God no longer loves them, and that he will never forgive them. This feeling is very real on one level. But the reality is that God showers his love and mercy upon all broken hearts. This chapter explores what might be interfering with your relationship with God—and how to reconnect with him.

Having an abortion is a total shock—physically, spiritually, emotionally, and psychologically. Afterward, a woman may isolate herself emotionally from other people and from God by withdrawing into her interior world and no longer reaching out to others. This isolation may result from physical trauma or from feelings of guilt, shame, low self-esteem, or a fear of being found out. What happened to Allison illustrates this reality:

❧

Allison considered herself a faithful follower of Jesus until her world fell apart. She gave in to the pressure of her boyfriend, who wanted her to have an abortion after she found out she was pregnant. They were planning to get married in two years. Having just completed her third year of college, she wanted to finish and go on to law school. So she was in turmoil about having a child.

She did not believe in abortion and wanted to follow God's ways. Yet her boyfriend pressured her very much and even threatened to leave her if she did not follow his wishes. And what about her own plans to move on to a career of her own? Allison used to be strong, but now she was full of confusion and heartache. She dared not tell her family or her friends, feeling she would be disgraced. Fear kept her from reaching out for help, from giving herself time to consider the child first, and from accepting motherhood.

Caving in to the pressure, Allison went against her own strong beliefs. After the abortion, she felt very different inside. "Who am I?" Allison asked herself. She felt that she had forever severed her relationship with God. "God will never forgive me for this," she told herself. She lapsed into depression and stopped seeing her friends. Her boyfriend did not understand this change. He broke up with Allison three months later. Then she felt more alienated than ever.

❖⌘❖⌘❖

The feeling that God has abandoned you can lead to feelings of terror, hopelessness, despair, and even thoughts of suicide (see Chapter 2 about other aftereffects). These anxieties may arise out of a self-imposed isolation. That is why it is so important for you to come into the light of God's love. He knows everything about you. God looks on you with great love, and he wants to heal you. God does not condemn you, so please do not condemn yourself. The mercy of God calls to you.

God created you in love. His love is constant and unconditional. His love for you has never stopped. God *is* love! Tragedy, sorrow, sin, weakness, and mistakes do not stop God from loving you. Think of the person you love most deeply in this world. Can you imagine that your love for this person would ever stop? Even in your weakness, even with hurts and pain, love does not end. Just imagine the perfect, endless love of God! God wants you to be whole, to be happy, to be healthy, and to have the joy of relationships with others.

You can turn away from God and decide to live without accepting God's offer of love. God gives us free will to make our own decisions—otherwise, his love and our own would not be true. If you feel distant from God, it is not because God wants you to be apart from him. The decision to come to God is yours to make.

Perhaps you have had two or three abortions. Healing can still be yours. Each abortion adds another layer of trauma, and it is important to work through each abortion, to reconnect with each child. Everything is possible for God and with God. Courage—walk into this light! Do not be afraid! You are not alone on this journey. Scripture says that the Divine Physician will heal all your ills: "What will separate us from the love of Christ? Will anguish, or distress, or persecution, or famine, or nakedness, or peril, or the sword? . . . For I am convinced that neither death, nor life, nor angels, nor principalities, nor present things, nor future things, nor powers, nor height, nor depth, nor any other creature will be able to separate us from the love of God in Christ Jesus our Lord" (Rom 8:35, 38–39).

So be gentle with yourself. Be kind to yourself. Your heart is in great sorrow. You may have decided to have an abortion while under great pressure from others, from a doctor, from time and timing, and from many other factors. The sorrow you have for your action is a sign that you would choose not to do this again. Exploring these factors helps you to know yourself better. Knowing your strengths and weaknesses is part of the lifetime journey of growing in maturity. This knowledge can help you to make healthier decisions in the future and grow closer to the people you love.

An abortion decision does not happen in isolation. Women who have had earlier traumas in their lives, such as rape or any type of childhood abuse, are already dealing with difficulties that may not have been resolved. Those factors make it harder to make other serious decisions with clarity—indeed, unresolved and unhealed pain can lead to other unhealthy decisions. As psychiatrist Bessel Van der Kolk says of trauma victims, "The trauma that started 'out there' is now played out on the battlefield of their own bodies, usually without a conscious connection between what happened back then and what is going on right now inside."[1]

The past cannot be changed. To learn from the past is a great gift. God brings good out of every situation in our lives. Christ redeems every sorrow. God and God alone is the one to judge the guilt of our sins. We *must* judge the morality of *actions*—whether an action is wrong or right, good or evil—but *not* judge the extent of the subjective guilt of a soul. No one has the right to judge the state of a person's soul. God alone knows our hearts, and he knows what factors influenced the important decisions in our lives. Saint Paul even says that we cannot judge ourselves: "It does not concern me in the least that I be judged by you or any human tribunal; I do not even pass judgment on myself; . . . the one who judges me is the Lord. Therefore, do not make any judgment before the appointed time, until the Lord comes, for he will bring to light what is hidden in darkness and will manifest the motives of our hearts" (1 Cor 4:3, 4–5).

Here is where the "truth will set you free" (Jn 8:32). The very point of freedom is found when you can be honest

---

1. Bessel A. Van der Kolk, *The Body Keeps the Score: Brain, Mind, and Body in the Healing of Trauma* (New York: Viking, 2014), 68.

with yourself before God about the extent, on some level, to which you agreed to the decision to abort your child (even if you felt pressured by others). New life comes from accepting the truth deep within yourself. Jesus tells us, "If you remain in my word, you will truly be my disciples, and you will know the truth, and the truth will set you free" (Jn 8:31–32). This is a key place where Jesus restores your total being to the land of the living, from life in the shadows to soaking in the light of truth, the light of life, the place of newfound joy where you can breathe freely. Arriving at the truth helps you to take responsibility for your decisions, and not to remain in victim mode or blame others.

True, it is not easy to accept certain realities about yourself or others—but truth and mercy are the keys, the answers you need to end your anguish and isolation. The purpose of facing the truth is not to condemn yourself, but to have compassion for yourself. *You have already suffered more than you need to.* Come to the arms of Jesus and find rest and peace. You will at times continue to grieve, but you will do so in a manner that will not lead to depression or isolation. Your grief will lead you to remember your child with great love. The missing pieces can be put together. Cloudy or distorted thinking can give way to clarity.

In working with so many brave women over the years, hearing the sorrow in their hearts and the suffering in their lives, I always think that the suffering of losing a child through abortion is perhaps one of the deepest of all sufferings.

The good news is that the gift of new life will flower in you through this process. It is the new life that is a gift to you from our loving God.

This flowering of new life is precisely why I stress the need to be gentle with yourself. Take this at a pace that will not overwhelm you. This important balance is stated by Father Mannion in discussing ways counselors can help women who have had an abortion:

> There may be the danger to be "over-compassionate," and minimize the gravity of the situation. A life has been lost. A child has been destroyed. We don't make excuses for her mistake or decision. We try to understand it, but not rationalize it. . . . To give her a cop-out, an escape from dealing with the reality of what she has done will not help her. The reality of what she has done must be named and understood if true reconciliation is to take place. Let her continue to deal with the anger and work it through. . . . We seek to confront and conquer the past, not avoid it. The goal is to help this woman, a friend, to cope.[2]

---

2. Mannion, *Abortion & Healing*, 80–81.

These are powerful words to absorb and take to heart.

The purpose of guilt is to bring us to the realization that we are on the wrong path, on a destructive path—that we have sinned, or that we are not in right relationship. Guilt may help us to realize the need to turn around, and then it is essential to let go of these powerful feelings; otherwise, they may lead to self-harm or harm to others. They become extra baggage that weighs a person down. The right attitude at this time is to have great hope in the living God of love and mercy.

Fear of Punishment

One serious irrational belief is thinking that anything bad that happens after an abortion is a punishment from God, especially if you have subsequently lost another child through miscarriage or if you are now infertile. This false belief can arise out of unresolved guilt. What may feel like punishment is really God calling you to a deeper relationship with him and to greater holiness. God desires you to be whole: "With age-old love I have loved you; / so I have kept my mercy toward you. / Again I will build you, and you shall stay built" (Jer 31:3–4). "For it is loyalty that I desire, not sacrifice. . ." (Hos 6:6). Here is an example of a woman who struggled with fear of punishment:

❖❖❖❖❖

Heidi is now married and the mother of two living children. When she was a single woman, her first pregnancy ended in abortion. She had been in a destructive relationship; her boyfriend was verbally abusive and often belittled her. He often threatened that if she did not use birth control and then got pregnant he would leave her. Somehow the birth control failed, but Heidi was not strong enough to tell her boyfriend that she was pregnant. She went on her own and had an abortion, never telling him. Afterward, she began to hate this man, as she realized he really did not care about her well-being. She was tired of the abuse and eventually broke up with him. She felt empty inside and regretted sacrificing her child for this man.

Heidi later sought out counseling, which helped to build her self-esteem, but she never talked about the abortion. Heidi met the man she eventually married and was able to have a healthy marriage. However, a second pregnancy ended in miscarriage. Heidi believed that God took her second child as a punishment for her earlier abortion. She felt she was undeserving to be a mother. Over time, as she processed her past and grew closer to God, Heidi began to realize that God is loving and that he was not punishing her. Heidi experienced peace by letting go of this false belief. With the two children she is raising, she is now able to experience the joys of motherhood without being weighed down by guilt. She now has the capacity to be fully present to her children and to her husband. This means that she is able to enjoy life in the present moment, to laugh, to embrace, to love, to rejoice in blessings, and to enjoy being around other people, especially her family. Heidi's husband and children benefit from her healing.

❖≫⌘≪❖

This fear of being punished can have an adverse effect on how you relate to your children. You may become overly protective, or you may not be able to bond in a healthy way. Then your children suffer. Chapter 7, on relationships, will say more about this. But for now, it is important to understand how fear stunts growth in your relationship with God.

To accept the reality that every person is a sinner is part of the walk in humility. For each of to accept that "*I am a sinner*" is even more difficult. To look at Jesus on the Cross can bring hope and a sense of the great love that

God has for you in giving his Son over to death to bring us to life. Father Richard Veras states this in a clear way:

> And now, after everything we have done, we ask forgiveness. Who do we think we are?! We are those for whom Jesus died. He died so that when we repent and seek forgiveness, the well of his mercy will always be open and full. So often we are afraid that reestablishing a relationship with someone we have wronged is hypocritical; but Christians call this reconciliation. How many friendships have ended because one who has betrayed will not forgive himself and so will not allow the other to forgive him? This is the story of Judas. Let us rather follow Peter. He is absent from the way of the cross, but he leads the Church in the way of repentance. Peter's life and preaching feed us by witnessing to Christ's infinite mercy.[3]

Judas was not able to accept Christ's mercy and forgiveness. This led to his self-destruction. Saint Peter also sinned, yet he was able to repent and let God's mercy change him. This helped Saint Peter to understand the weaknesses in others and to be compassionate toward them. In the same way, accepting our sinfulness is part of accepting our humanity, and accepting our humanity is

---

3. Richard Veras, "Via Crucis: The Way of the Cross," *Magnificat* 16, no. 1 (Holy Week, 2014): 176.

the royal road of grace that we walk on our way to our true home in God. Grace builds on nature. Jesus said to the woman caught in adultery: "'Woman, where are they? Has no one condemned you?' She replied, 'No one, sir.' Then Jesus said, 'Neither do I condemn you. Go, [and] from now on do not sin any more'" (Jn 8:10–11).

Right Relationship with God

If your relationship with God is strong, I encourage you to continue to trust in his promises. If you feel distant from God, I hope you will discover that he is very close to you. To be in right relationship with God is the first step in restoration. His grace will help you to be open to forgiveness and to let go of all that hinders you from peaceful living. Remember the Good News: Jesus died for you to free you from sin, to remove the roadblocks that keep you from experiencing freedom and peace. To believe you can never be forgiven can be a kind of false pride or a temptation. Give up your fear and find reconciliation with God. Then you will find your true self.

You may have difficulty in relating to God as Father, if the relationship with your earthly father was difficult or even painful. But God the Father is always faithful. His love is ever steady as he provides for all that you need. Accepting God as your true Father can help heal the relationship with your earthly father. You may find it helpful to explore this area in more depth during this time in your life.

Perhaps you are angry at God. "Where were you, God, when I was making this anguished decision? Why didn't you rescue me? Why didn't you send me someone to help me?" You may feel that God abandoned you during that time in your life. The cry of your heart is a very human experience, as we read in the book of Psalms: "How long, LORD? Will you utterly forget me? / How long will you hide your face from me? / How long must I carry sorrow in my soul, / grief in my heart day after day?" (Ps 13:2–3). These and similar questions you might ask yourself are important to explore. God can handle your anger, and he will answer your questions.

To sort through these questions and feelings will help you to realize that God *was* there at the time. You might have pushed God away in your panic. Your defense mechanisms might have prevented you from focusing on the presence and the voice of God. Do not be afraid to explore these areas with a Catholic–Christian counselor who understands the importance of drawing closer to God at this time. At a pace that is comfortable for you, you move to greater freedom, one step at a time.

It is okay to express angry feelings you may have toward God. You may want to write God a letter to pour out the emotions in your heart. Then you can write a letter from God to you. These are very powerful exercises to seek the heart of God and to place your own heart in his. This process can open up space inside you to give the anger a safe expression and to let in healing love. This encourages facing all parts of your life with honesty. God knows you better than you know yourself. This process leads to a greater self-knowledge and acceptance.

Establishing and building any relationship requires two-way communication. This is true between two people. It is also the way to be in friendship with God. Taking time to talk with God and to listen to him is the first step. Take quiet time away from others, away from the phone, internet, and other distractions. In the silence, you can learn to recognize God's voice and experience the depth of his tender care for you.

Start with just a few minutes of prayer each day and build from there. Speaking with God is really very simple. Love does not complicate matters. You can speak to God as you would speak to your very best friend. Talking to God *is* prayer. Open your heart to the one who loves you beyond measure. Jesus is waiting to embrace you. Sit in a quiet place and listen to God tell you how much he loves you. Open your Bible and read one of the psalms. These ancient prayers are as relevant today as they were when they were written, three thousand years ago, because they are prayers of the heart, expressing the joys and sorrows of living life. Jesus is waiting for you to take one step toward him, and he will run the rest of the way to embrace you. Jesus invites you—he never forces the relationship. This gift of freedom is the greatest gift God gives you.

God's Forgiveness

Many avenues of spiritual support are available to you. If you do not have a religious affiliation, just praying and reading the Bible can be very helpful at this time. Find someone with whom you can share your questions. If you do have a church community, use the prayer traditions in the Church you belong to. For Catholics, the Sacrament of Reconciliation is a very helpful way to experience the peace and healing that Christ gives through the Church. If your diocese has a Project Rachel ministry, ask them to refer you to a priest who gives dedicated time to abortion healing ministry and who can help you more fruitfully receive the Sacrament of Reconciliation.

Some women have said they have difficulty confessing the sin of abortion to a priest. The reality is that

Christ meets us in the sacrament. It is Christ who for-gives; it is Christ who heals and brings the gift of whole-ness to us. Christ is present in the person of the priest. Confession is absolutely confidential. Rest assured that the priest cannot repeat what he hears in the sacrament. In fact, priests have told me that they forget afterward all that they heard—this is a gift from God. Nevertheless, some women feel more comfortable going to confession to a priest at another parish. If you haven't been to con-fession for a long time, simply tell the priest that and ask him to help you make an honest confession. This psalm can encourage you:

> Blessed is the one whose fault is removed,
>   whose sin is forgiven. . . .
>
> Because I kept silent, my bones wasted away;
>   I groaned all day long.
> For day and night your hand was heavy upon me;
>   my strength withered as in dry summer heat.
>
> Then I declared my sin to you;
>   my guilt I did not hide.
> I said, "I confess my transgression to the Lord,"
>   and you took away the guilt of my sin. . . .
>
> You are my shelter; you guard me from distress;
>   with joyful shouts of deliverance you surround
>   me. (Ps 32:1, 3–5, 7)

Speaking your sins out loud to another person and receiving forgiveness allows healing to take place. To be able to confess in the confidential setting of the sacrament brings great relief and calm to mind and soul. Burdens lift. The spirit soars. The power of this special grace helps a person to move forward to the unique life Christ offers. Again, this is a matter of trusting God, of believing that God's promises are true and lasting. A Catholic does have an obligation to tell a priest about the sin of abortion in the Sacrament of Reconciliation, in order to receive absolution, which means God forgives the sin. The Catholic is then in the state of grace—of being in right relationship with God—and can then receive the Sacrament of the Eucharist. If you are of another Christian denomination, or another religion entirely, seek out a religious leader you trust to confide your sorrow and repentance, if you so desire.

Because of the trauma that may occur after an abortion, some women suffer from the anxiety-driven compulsion to confess this sin over and over again. This may present a psychological as well as a spiritual difficulty. Once a sin is confessed and absolution is given, the Church teaches there is no reason to confess this sin again: "As far as the east is from the west, / so far has he removed our sins from us" (Ps 103:12). Isaiah writes, "Come now, let us set things right, / says the LORD: / Though your sins be like scarlet, / they may become white as snow; / Though they be red like crimson, / they may become white as wool" (Is 1:18).

Again, the Sacrament of Reconciliation is an invitation to take God at his word and accept the gift of restoration. The priest will give you a penance to complete. Penance usually involves prayers to say or a work of mercy to do in order to make amends to God. It is not meant as a punishment, but rather as a way to turn your heart to God. Then you may move forward, entrusting your soul to God. Accepting this reassurance from God can help you remove any compulsion to confess the same sin repeatedly.

Other Ways of Healing

In addition to praying, receiving the sacraments, reading Scripture, and finding a spiritual guide, you can do other things to encourage peace and progress. You might find it helpful to keep a journal of your thoughts and feelings. Expressing your thoughts and feelings through art or a craft can also help you connect with different parts of your brain. If you find expression in dance, this may also be a powerful tool. Write a song or listen to a song that has meaning for you. Write a poem or a story.

In some way, be creative. Discover the mode of expression that helps you to get to the depths and adds an important dimension during your unique inner travels. These ideas are ways of getting these expressions outside of yourself, where you can see them in a different perspective. These artistic expressions are just for you, so don't censor your thoughts and feelings—especially when dealing with anger.

Are you searching for relief from running away, running from God, and running from your true self? You are beautiful, gracious, and lovely! These words from the Song of Songs are addressed to *you:*

> My lover speaks and says to me,
>> "Arise, my friend, my beautiful one,
>> and come!
> For see, the winter is past,
>> the rains are over and gone.
> The flowers appear on the earth,
>> the time of pruning the vines has come,
>> and the song of the turtledove is heard in our land. . . .
>
> "How beautiful you are, my friend,
>> how beautiful you are!" (Sg 2:10–12; 4:1)

We are more than our sins, greater than our mistakes. One sin, one mistake—or even many—does not define a person. You are a person of infinite worth and value, because your Savior and brother, Jesus Christ, loved you so much that he gave his life for you on the Cross. You share in his Resurrection as well as his Cross, and his gift to you is new life! May you discover this gift.

Paths to Avoid

After an abortion, some women continue to go to church but still believe they are unworthy of God's mercy. They stop receiving the sacraments and drop out of activities they were involved in. Some women stop attending church altogether, or they may go to a church of another denomination. Others may stop all practice of any faith and might stop believing in God. These unfortunate decisions lead to more desolation. If you have made such a wrong turn in the road, Jesus will help you to get back on the path of life.

A more radical reaction to post-abortion fallout is that some women become involved in New Age practices, superstitions, or even the occult. These occult/New Age practices are very popular in our culture today, and this reaction may be driven by guilt, anxiety, and false beliefs. But these practices are very dangerous to the soul, because a person can get involved with evil spirits without realizing the danger. This will only lead a person into greater depression and/or anxiety and greater fear, not to true healing. Vulnerable people are often the victims of these false claims of healings, which can cause more harm because they are not of the spirit of God.

God doesn't want anyone to go down this destructive path. If you are involved in such practices, the best step is to speak to a priest, a spiritual director, or a Catholic or Christian counselor. Any of these people can help you to learn how to discern when God is acting in your life or when evil forces are working to influence you. This is a safer way to the truth than navigating this passage on your own.

The healing process has many layers. It takes time to sort through false beliefs and to be able to accept the truth. Courage, patience, and honesty are important tools you can use to accept God's Word as lasting and true. Anything that gives you an uncomfortable or unsettled gut feeling can be harmful. Any practice that is secretive and leads you into greater darkness is harmful. Come into the light. Accept God's love, mercy, and forgiveness. He has created you for friendship with him, and no sin can separate you from God unless you choose not to accept his offer. Jesus said, "I came into the world as light, so that everyone who believes in me might not remain in darkness" (Jn 12:46).

Another trap that prevents healing is feeling as if you must atone for (make up for the loss of) this child by getting overly involved in helping others. For example, perhaps you feel compelled to be involved in pro-life work such as helping at a pregnancy care center. But Jesus Christ already made atonement when he offered his life on the Cross for you and for all of us. He already paid the price.

What God asks of you instead is to work on integrating into your life all you are learning, so that you are whole and full of joy. Your desire to change and to be whole is pleasing to God. Then you become once again a person fully alive, one who expresses the joy of the gift of life in all you do. What greater gift can you give to the world than letting Jesus shine through you! To accept this free gift of God may be difficult for you, but it is crucial to do so. Otherwise you may become very tired trying to achieve what is not within your ability to achieve.

What a marvelous God! He gives you unconditional love, forgiveness, and atonement. In the future, you will be able to discern if God wants you to volunteer to help others. This will then be an act of self-giving, not an act of compulsion to change what cannot be changed.

In closing this chapter, I again encourage you to develop your relationship with God so that you discover the fullness of who you are in his love. This will open your heart to a true knowledge of the love of God, and a true understanding of your dignity and worth as a person, as a daughter of God. False beliefs and fears will be replaced with hope, wisdom, and understanding. Love and truth will strengthen you to accept the forgiveness and mercy that are yours in Christ Jesus. This will open you to work toward forgiving others and yourself.

Scriptures Meditations on God's Love

- ❖ Genesis 1:26–31
- ❖ Exodus 14:13–14
- ❖ John 8:1–11
- ❖ 2 Corinthians 4:6–10

Reflection Questions

- ❖ Was there a time when you felt close to God? Think about this experience. How did God help you at that time?
- ❖ What would you like God to help you with now?
- ❖ What is your relationship with God like?

Tips for Family Members and Friends

- ❖ If your loved one has been away from the practice of her faith, you can gently invite her back. Don't push. She needs to move forward at a pace that is comfortable for her.

◈   Pray often for your loved one to know God's healing love and mercy. Your prayers are powerful.

◈   Remember that God loves this person even more than you do and desires her restoration to health even more than you do.

CHAPTER 4

Anger and Forgiveness

"And forgive us our sins,
for we ourselves forgive everyone in debt to us."

Luke 11:4

Accepting God's mercy is like welcoming a gentle spring breeze that refreshes every part of your being. Freedom brings a joy that opens your heart to the beauty and renewal of each new day. You are once again able to enjoy feeling alive. The awesome gift of accepting God's forgiveness opens new possibilities in your life for renewal of relationships.

Yet you might still harbor strong anger toward people who were involved in the decision to abort your child. It is vital for you to examine each of these relationships. The goal is to be able to offer mercy to each person through prayer (it may not be possible or wise to do this face to face with each person). Doing so frees your own energies for developing positive relationships, working on goals, and engaging in life-giving activities.

Sometimes we hold on to negative emotions so long that we get used to them. But anger and lack of forgiveness can weigh you down, like carrying a heavy suitcase. How does this baggage make you feel? Does it slow you down? Does it make you tired? Your anger may be justified. Yet acknowledging these feelings, working through them, and letting them go brings freedom to the depth of your soul and improves your overall well-being. Picture yourself opening that suitcase and taking out unneeded items. Pick up the suitcase again. Is it lighter? Do you really need to carry such a heavy load? Imagine deciding to walk away from the suitcase. How does that feel? Do you feel even lighter? Do you want this freedom?

In the Our Father, we ask God to forgive us in the measure that we forgive others. That is a powerful responsibility. If God has forgiven you, it is now time for you to forgive others. The prophet Jeremiah writes: "Heal me, LORD, that I may be healed; / save me, that I may be saved, / for you are my praise" (Jer 17:14). Each of us is influenced by many relationships, both past and present. A decision not to accept the child in the womb is never made in isolation. An important part of your work is therefore to forgive others—a difficult phase, but one that is so very important to regaining your freedom.

So why bring up all these memories and rehash what cannot change your past decision? Precisely because the memories are there, the emotions are there, the pain and suffering are there. To give them a voice, to shed light on the dark corners of your heart, to open the infection to the light of fresh air can bring so much of your pain and darkness to closure. Giving voice to your anger helps you regain your own voice, so you may learn more about your true self and gain confidence. Even if you are no longer in contact with any of the people you are angry at (or if someone is now deceased), you can find peace for yourself. By talking with a trusted person, and engaging in prayerful reflection, you can release your negative emotions and find stability and joy. The Gospel tells us: "Be merciful, just as [also] your Father is merciful. Stop judging and you will not be judged. Stop condemning and you will not be condemned. Forgive and you will be forgiven. Give and gifts will be given to you; a good measure, packed together, shaken down, and overflowing, will be poured into your lap. For the measure with which you measure will in return be measured out to you" (Lk 6:36–38).

Denial of anger can be a way to protect yourself from pain.

Perhaps you are not even aware of your anger. If you think you are not angry at anyone, make a list of all the people involved in the abortion decision. Take time listing each person. If feelings and thoughts of anger begin to bubble up, pay attention. Give these thoughts and feelings a voice, so you can deal with them in a healthy way. Take time with this process. Don't force it. The Lord will reveal to you the people and situations that you need to revisit with his help.

For example, perhaps you really did not want the abortion, but your boyfriend, husband, or parent(s) pressured you. Maybe fear of disrupting your own goals put more pressure on you. The staff at the abortion facility might not have given you all the information you needed to make an informed decision. The nurse or abortionist may have been very cold toward you and in a hurry to get you out of the building. You may have had physical problems afterward, but the abortion facility would not see you for follow-up. Perhaps a friend betrayed you. Perhaps you were feeling inadequate to be a parent due to your own parents' inadequate skills, which caused you pain as a child.

This list-making exercise is for your well-being. Take quiet time to pray. Be honest with yourself. Then look again at the list of people and identify those with whom you are angry. (You may add to the list as time goes on.) Take the first name and begin to review your feelings toward this person. You might find it helpful to write down your thoughts and exactly what feelings you are experiencing. Be specific as to what you are angry about. How did this person disappoint or betray you? The more you can pinpoint your reasons for your hurt feelings, the better you can understand how this hurt affected your own decision. Don't censor your writing—express yourself honestly.

Working toward forgiving others does not mean that you need to speak to each person or renew each relationship. Time has moved on, and it may not be healthy or practical to tell each person directly that you forgive him or her. Reconciliation between two people is not always possible; and to contact a former boyfriend or spouse could be disruptive to everyone concerned. But forgiveness is always possible. You can resolve the anger within yourself through praying and through speaking with the person who is guiding you through the healing. Through prayer and God's grace, you can forgive each person who hurt you and go forward in peace.

Your inner voice may be saying, "I can never forgive him"; "I can never forgive her." This is the time to remember how much mercy God has shown you. If God has forgiven you, it is possible for you to pardon others. Remember that Jesus said, "Blessed are the merciful, / for they will be shown mercy" (Mt 5:7).

Forgiveness is not a one-time event, either. You may sincerely forgive an individual for a time. Then memories may flood back and cause the angry feelings to return. This presents you with an opportunity to forgive again, to lift this person up to God in prayer. When God asks us to love our neighbor, he means we should wish the best for each person. Understanding why you feel as you do about a particular situation or person doesn't necessarily change your feelings—but it can help you get better control of your responses to these feelings.[1] Being able to name your anger is a way to gain control over your emotions. When you control your emotions, they no longer control you.

Pay attention to how your body reacts as you experience these feelings of anger. Are your muscles tense, is your breathing shallow and fast, is your stomach in knots? Unresolved anger can cause physical ailments such as high blood pressure or headaches. If your emotions are too

---

1. See Van der Kolk, *Body Keeps the Score*, 205.

strong and cause you more stress, come back to this exercise later. Take a break.

Find healthy outlets to release negative emotions, instead of taking your anger out on people you love. For example, draw your angry feelings. Write angry words and put them in a jar; then, at the end of the day, tear up the papers in the jar and throw them away. Physical exercise can help relieve the stress of anger. Do housework or yard-work to release your pent-up emotions. Work out at the gym, join an exercise class, or take up a new hobby. Do something that gives you an outside interest and increases your joy in living.

Most likely, you are taking your anger out on yourself, too. If you repress this anger, you might release it inappropriately in a way that you may regret. Displaced anger can hurt those who are innocent. The psychiatrist Van der Kolk explains, "Most human beings simply cannot tolerate being disengaged from others for any length of time. People who cannot connect through work, friendships, or family usually find other ways of bonding, as through illnesses, lawsuits, or family feuds."[2] That is why making a list of each person you are angry with will help you focus

---

2. Van der Kolk, *Body Keeps the Score*, 115.

your energy toward those you need to forgive. The "revenge" of anger only puts you in an emotional prison while having no effect on the other person. This may be a time for you to act with kindness and patience toward yourself.

Feelings of shame can prevent you from forgiving others. If you suffer with low self-esteem, you may mistakenly feel that you deserve whatever happened, even if another person was also at fault. These negative thoughts and feelings may have been deeply ingrained for many years. This shame points to another important area of your life that you might explore: to be able to experience your self-worth and dignity as a gift from God. Accepting God's forgiveness, forgiving others, and forgiving yourself are all interrelated. Perhaps you need to look at your own role in your lack of forgiveness. It is important to ask yourself, "Did I do something to contribute to my being angry at this person?" Because of your own role in the abortion decision, you might find it difficult to let go of anger toward others if you haven't yet forgiven yourself.

If you have been deeply hurt or betrayed by someone you trusted, you might find it very difficult to trust again. Examining each reason for anger at each person on your list will help you to sort out false beliefs from the truth. Perhaps you were in an unhealthy relationship, for example. Instead of putting yourself down for making poor choices, examine the reasons for your choices. You can learn from the past to make wiser decisions and to strengthen your confidence. When you can be honest about the reality of each relationship, the truth will surface in your heart, bringing you freedom.

Forgiving others also breaks the chains of self-isolation. Isolation may happen because of the trauma of the abortion itself, because of feelings of shame, or because of numbing or burying your emotions. As Van der Kolk points out, "Being traumatized is not just an issue of being stuck in the past; it is just as much a problem of not being fully alive in the present."[3] As you gently explore the negative emotions and gradually release them, spaces open within yourself to make room for other people. Experiences of love, joy, peace, and safety replace anger and shame. You will once again be able to express these positive emotions to the people you love, including yourself.

Other obstacles might prevent your forgiving other people. Again, an abortion decision does not happen in isolation from other events in your life. Lack of forgiveness may be compounded by unhealed hurts from your

---

3. Ibid., 221.

past, such as childhood sexual abuse, physical abuse, or neglect. Difficulty in forgiving may be complicated by a series of betrayals, disappointments, or losses. These obstacles can be named and worked on, one at a time. If you experienced trauma prior to the abortion, such as rape or incest, it is important for you to work on healing that area first. Unhealed trauma leaves a person more vulnerable to future trauma and the possibility of making inadequate decisions to protect oneself: "Traumatized people become stuck, stopped in their growth because they can't integrate new experiences into their lives. . . . Being traumatized means continuing to organize your life as if the trauma were still going on—unchanged and immutable—as every new encounter or event is contaminated by the past."[4] But as you work through and remove each obstacle, you gain greater interior openness.

Defense Mechanisms

Defense mechanisms can keep you from looking at your own role in a negative situation. They begin as a way to provide yourself with emotional safety after a traumatic

---

4. Ibid., 53.

event, in order not to be overwhelmed by the reality and consequences of the event. These defenses protect you for some time, and then they begin to break down. When this happens, it is time to take an honest look at yourself and develop healthy ways to cope with reality. Over time, defense mechanisms can even create a maze of lies, misunderstandings, avoidance of the truth, or avoidance of being your true self. By sidestepping an examination of your role in the abortion decision, you hide from the truth.

But the truth is inside you. Facing it brings relief. Finding a way out of the maze takes time, patience, courage, and great love. Work on these defenses at a comfort level that brings you peace, not anxiety. The prophet Isaiah reassures us:

> Is this not, rather, the fast that I choose:
> > releasing those bound unjustly,
> > untying the thongs of the yoke;
> Setting free the oppressed,
> > breaking off every yoke? . . .
> Then your light shall break forth like the dawn,
> > and your wound shall quickly be healed. . . .
> Then your light shall rise in the darkness,
> > and your gloom shall become like midday;
> Then the Lord will guide you always
> > and satisfy your thirst in parched places,

  will give strength to your bones
 And you shall be like a watered garden,
   like a flowing spring whose waters never fail.
    (Is 58:6, 8, 10–11)

Yokes are things that bind or burden you, just like the yoke that binds oxen to a plow. What yokes keep you bound inwardly? What is oppressing your inner self? Numerous psychological and spiritual defense mechanisms keep a person from facing the truth. Now is the time to begin to unfasten these yokes.

The rest of this chapter will look at four defense mechanisms: denial, rationalization, projection, and displacement. Identifying them will help you to understand how you may be inhibiting your own healing. Jesus said: "Come to me, all you who labor and are burdened, and I will give you rest. Take my yoke upon you and learn from me, for I am meek and humble of heart; and you will find rest for yourselves. For my yoke is easy, and my burden light" (Mt 11:28–30).

Denial enables a person to downplay the seriousness of an action or to not accept the reality of what happened. A young woman who agrees to an abortion to please her boyfriend may be in denial about whether he truly loves her. She may be angry afterward that this boyfriend did not protect her and their child, especially if he breaks off the relationship after the abortion. She might find it easy, then, to slip into changing the story of what really happened, as the following woman's struggle illustrates:

❖⁀❀⁀❖

Yvette was a single woman whose career was the main focus of her life. When she discovered she was pregnant for the first time in her late thirties, she didn't want to believe it, so she just let time go by. She waited until her fifth month of pregnancy to go to the doctor. She did not believe in abortion but was influenced by lack of interest on the part of the father of her baby and by her own fears of raising a child alone. She did not even consider adoption.

Yvette was afraid to trust in God. She decided she would go through with an abortion. After she had delayed so long, she now made a rushed decision and was scheduled to have an abortion at the hospital, because the baby was close to the seventh month of gestation. The so-called support staff offered to have a "remembrance" ceremony and even arranged for this mother to see and hold her dead baby, which she agreed to do. Years later, when Yvette was relating this story in a counseling session, she thought about

this planned grieving ceremony as almost normal-
izing the situation, as if the baby had died of natural
causes instead of from an abortion. This mistaken
normalization enabled Yvette to easily sink into denial about her decision to end the life of her child.
Her denial was deep and not easy to break though.
Yvette knew in her heart that the baby did not die
of natural causes, but she was reluctant to face this
truth, even though facing it would then open the
door to her healing.

❖⤙❖⤙❖

Rationalization is similar to denial; it means to make
up excuses instead of accepting the truth. For example,
consider a woman who has an abortion because her parents have told her they will no longer pay for her college
tuition if she has the baby. She may go on to rationalize her
role in the decision by saying she had no other option.

Projection, another defense mechanism, allows a person to attribute negative emotions to another person,
instead of acknowledging these emotions in oneself. A
woman may feel ashamed of her own past abortion—but
instead of acknowledging this self-shame, she looks down
on someone else who has made the same decision.

Finally, *displacement* occurs when a person takes out anger on others instead of making internal changes. A woman may still harbor anger toward her boyfriend who left her after she had an abortion five years before. She might take out that past anger on her husband, instead of working on forgiving her former boyfriend.

Such unhealed hurts can block the joy of the present moment or interfere with your life's vocation. The purpose of this deep work of self-examination is to transform your entire person. It is like keeping the weeds out of the garden of your soul. Saint Paul tells us, "Rejoice in the Lord always. I shall say it again: rejoice! . . . The Lord is near. Have no anxiety at all, but in everything, by prayer and petition, with thanksgiving, make your requests known to God. Then the peace of God that surpasses all understanding will guard your hearts and minds in Christ Jesus" (Phil 4:4, 5–7).

God asks you to forgive others as he forgives you. This act offers freedom to the other person on the spiritual level. To pardon others allows freedom to flow again in your own life—perhaps you will experience this freedom for the first time. Drop the extra baggage so you can use your arms to hug those you love instead of keeping them at a distance.

Scripture Meditations on Forgiveness

❖ Matthew 7:2–5

❖ Matthew 7:7–8

❖ Luke 15:21–24

❖ Luke 6:43–48

Reflection Questions

❖ How do you usually deal with your anger?

❖ Are you afraid of your anger? If so, how can you deal with it in a healthy way?

❖ Do you acknowledge a connection between releasing your anger and forgiving someone?

❖ Do you want to be free of anger? What can you do right now to move toward that goal?

❖ Do you use a defense mechanism to keep painful information out of your conscious mind? Does this help or hurt you? How can you resolve this difficulty?

❖ As you strive to forgive people who have hurt you, you will find freedom. Have you ever experienced this freedom? In what ways?

❖ You may need to forgive a person more than once if angry feelings begin to surface again. Be patient. Jesus will help you. Do you trust that he will?

Tips for Family Members and Friends

❖ Defense mechanisms can help protect us until we are strong enough to work on healing. These can't be removed quickly. We usually let go of them as we learn healthy ways to cope with the truth.

❖ Anger can be used to keep people at a safe emotional distance. You can model healthy coping skills to your loved one without directly speaking to her about her own difficulties.

❖ Are you angry at your loved one because she had an abortion? It is important to examine this. Your anger will not help her. She already feels bad enough about her decision and may struggle with low self-esteem. Instead, ask God to help free you from this anger. Your forgiveness, compassion, and mercy will then help her.

CHAPTER 5

Spiritual Relationship with Your Child

But this I will call to mind;
    therefore I will hope:
The LORD's acts of mercy are not exhausted,
    his compassion is not spent;
They are renewed each morning—
    great is your faithfulness!
The LORD is my portion, I tell myself,
    therefore I will hope in him.
The LORD is good to those who trust in him,
    to the one that seeks him;
It is good to hope in silence
        for the LORD's deliverance.

Lamentations 3:21–26

This path you are on requires great courage. The love in your heart is expanding, and hopefully you are living with greater serenity. Part of the work of healing your own broken heart and putting together all the pieces is connecting with your precious child on the spiritual level. From the moment of conception, a unique human person comes into existence, who has DNA totally different from anyone who has ever lived or will ever live. God gives an immortal soul to each individual at this same moment. The *Catechism of the Catholic Church* states: "In Sacred Scripture the term 'soul' often refers to human *life* or the entire human *person*. But 'soul' also refers to the inner-most aspect of man, that which is of greatest value in him, that by which he is most especially in God's image: 'soul' signifies the *spiritual principle* in man.¹

God has given the human person a dignity greater than all other created things.

The abortion industry often describes the infant in the womb as a "blob of tissue" or "not yet human." It does not use the word "child" or "baby" to describe this irreplaceable human being. That misuse of language seeks to take

---

1. *Catechism of the Catholic Church*, 2nd ed. (Washington, DC: United States Conference of Catholic Bishops—Liberia Editrice Vaticana, 1997), no. 363, italics original.

away the child's personhood. Human life has many stages of growth and development from conception to natural death. Each stage of life is sacred and precious, as the psalmist reminds us: "I praise you, because I am wonderfully made; / wonderful are your works! / My very self you know" (Ps 139:14).

Death does not end love. The love that you have always had for this child may be tucked away in a far corner of your mind and heart. As you grow in your relationship with God and become more able to accept your own dignity, you will be able to open your heart to give and receive love from your child. Do not be afraid. "Deep waters cannot quench love, / nor rivers sweep it away" (Sg 8:7). Your child loves you.

Over the years, women have asked me many questions about their children, often arising from internal fears. "Where is my baby now? What does my child think of me? If I move forward in healing, if I move on with my life, will I forget my child?" Such questions are all very legitimate to ask. As you face your anxieties and bring them to the light, peace will come to you. The Gospel of John reminds us, "For God so loved the world that he gave his only Son, so that everyone who believes in him might not perish but might have eternal life. For God did not send his Son into the world to condemn the world, but that the world might be saved through him. . . . But whoever lives the truth comes to the light" (Jn 3:16–17, 21).

If you wonder "Where is my baby now?" let these beautiful words of Saint Pope John Paul II console you:

> I would now like to say a special word to women who have had an abortion. The Church is aware of the many factors, which may have influenced your decision, and she does not doubt that in many cases it was a painful and even shattering decision. The wound in your heart may not yet have healed. Certainly what happened was and remains terribly wrong. But do not give in to discouragement and do not lose hope. Try rather to understand what happened and face it honestly. If you have not already done so, give yourselves over with humility and trust to repentance. The Father of mercies is ready to give you his forgiveness and his peace in the Sacrament of Reconciliation. *To the same Father and his mercy you can with sure hope entrust your child.* With the friendly and expert help and advice of other people, and as a result of your own painful experience, you can be among the most eloquent defenders of everyone's right to life. Through your commitment to life, whether by accepting the birth of other children or by welcoming and caring for those most in need of someone to be close to them, you will become promoters of a new way of looking at human life.[2] (Emphasis mine)

---

2. John Paul II, Encyclical *Evangelium vitae (The Gospel of Life)*, March 25, 1995, w2.vatican.va/content/john-paul-ii/en/encyclicals/documents/hf_jp-ii_enc_25031995_evangelium-vitae.html, no. 99.

Hopefully these words will help you to understand that your child rests in God.

Some women have shared with me that while praying, they imagine their child being held in the arms of Jesus. They may see the child as a baby, or as a young one running and laughing and then holding Jesus' hand. These images in prayer bring peace and hope to women who experience them. Perhaps you can ask Jesus to help you encounter the presence of your child during prayer.

Part of accepting the personhood of your child is to give your child a name. You may have a sense of whether your child is a boy or a girl. This naming is a gift from the Lord and has a timing that is up to God. God offers you this loving act of naming your child as a way to share in God's creativity. God has a name for your child—and as the mother, you may have an intuitive sense about this name. Naming is remembering. Naming is getting to know. This is accepting the humanity of your child.

Do you ask: "What does my child think about me?" Women express worries that their child may hate them, that the child will never forgive them, or that the child is lost to them forever. These deep fears are understandable, yet they can prevent healing.

Your child loves you now with an unconditional, eternal love. The bond between a mother and her child can never be broken. It is an eternal bond. Your child prays for you and forgives you. Your child is in total peace in God.

At the perfect time, God may allow you to experience the reality of this relationship. This is not something you can force. It is a gift from God, who knows exactly what you need as you grow in spiritual maturity. This calls to mind another woman who had such a tender experience of this gift from God, seemingly out of the blue:

❖⤙⤙❖❖⤙⤙❖

Mandy and her husband agreed to abort their third child early in the pregnancy. They had financial problems and one of their children had health problems. Mandy wanted this third child, but her husband was adamant that now was not the right time to have another child. She begged and pleaded for her husband to change his mind, but to no avail. Her husband threatened to divorce her. Mandy needed his financial help, especially the insurance to help with medical needs of their child who was ill. She was afraid to face life alone without him, so she caved in to his pressure.

They eventually divorced anyway, as the bond of trust between them had been broken. Mandy went for counseling ten years after this abortion, as the sorrow in her heart was too great for her to bear alone anymore. After many months and much hard work, Mandy was able to live with a greater peace in her life. It was, however, very difficult for her to accept that her third child could forgive her. It seemed impossible for her to accept that this child could love her after she had decided to not accept this child into her life. She could imagine on an intellectual level that all was okay with this child. But it was not easy for her to accept this in her heart.

One day, Mandy was sitting at the seashore by herself. She was enjoying the warm breeze and the gentle lull of the waves. Great peace filled her heart. Her mind began to drift to thoughts of her child with God. Then she had an experience of her child sitting beside her, taking her hand, and just being there in love. This experience was so real for her. The child did not speak; she was simply present in great love. Mandy's heart opened wide, and her doubts and anxieties drifted away with the gentle breeze. She knew in this instant that her child loved her, embraced her, and forgave her. The missing piece was now in place and her life was complete again, after ten painful years. The joy of this gift enabled her to relate at a deeper level with her two living children. Her heart was free to love with a deeper, purer love. This was a gift from God that she was so grateful to receive.

❧◈❧◈❧

An essential element in moving forward emotionally is linked to the area of grief. Some women express concern that they might forget the child if they heal from the painful memories of the abortion. They may want to keep everything the same—the memories, feelings, and reminders. A person can become stuck on the emotional level and find it difficult to let new experiences and relationships into his or her life. Please know that facing your sorrow will not cause you to forget your child. It will open your heart to a fuller love.

Complicated Grief

Certain conditions can lead to complicated grief, which adds more layers to the healing process. If a person does not grieve, it is difficult to find health and freedom. Even though grief is painful, it needs healthy outlets to free the person to move on to greater calm. Then the pain will subside. If this sounds like you, please remember that this process is meant to bring about relief. Please do not be hard on yourself. The purpose is to understand what is weighing you down, not to condemn yourself.

Complicated grief may occur in situations where there is no body to grieve over, when there is no grave to visit, when the death is sudden and/or violent, or when there is some level of participation in the death. It is not unusual for complicated grief to occur after an abortion.

Seeing the body of a dead loved one helps survivors to realize the reality of what has occurred. But there is no body to grieve over when someone dies in a fire, at sea, in war. Just so, there is no grave to visit, no burial, for the child who died in abortion. There is no place to go to grieve, no place for a memorial. When a baby or young child dies of natural causes, a funeral and burial can take place. Society does not acknowledge your grief in the case of abortion. It becomes easy to go into denial about the abortion, telling oneself instead that the baby died through miscarriage. Women may slip in and out of denial in the early stages of healing work. This is another reason why it is important to talk to someone you trust, so that you won't fool yourself.

And you can still have hope, because you can thoughtfully plan your own way to grieve in private. The response to the reality of having no grave to visit is to create your own memorial. You may create a unique place for remembrance in your own home or in your yard, such as planting a tree, making a special garden, or perhaps arranging a space of beauty inside your home to honor the memory of your child. You may plan a special prayer service or have a Mass of the Resurrection offered to honor the child. Invite people who are close to you and who have walked with you during this time, so you can grieve and rejoice in God's great mercy. There are memorial gardens specifically for children lost to abortion, where plaques or memorial trees can be purchased (see Appendix 3). Having a quiet remembrance each year on the child's likely birthday can help you to honor your child. You can come up with your own ideas that make this special for you.

A sudden and or violent death can also bring on complicated grief. Not having the time to say goodbye may lead to an unresolved relationship with the person who died. Most abortions occur within a week to ten days of finding out one is pregnant. This rushed decision leaves so many loose ends. The good news is that you can move beyond this phase of being stuck in grief.

Another factor in complicated grief occurs when someone participated on some level in the death of the loved one—which is the situation in a decision to have an abortion. These realities are difficult to face, yet facing the truth always brings freedom and relief. Invite Jesus to be with you during this moment. At the Last Supper, Jesus said: "Do not let your hearts be troubled. You have faith in God; have faith also in me" (Jn 14:1). Talk about this with your therapist or spiritual advisor so you receive the support you need. Let yourself cry, let yourself feel the sorrow and pain of having made that decision. Have compassion for yourself. This release of buried feelings and thoughts brings cleansing, just like a gentle rain can wash away heavy humidity and clear the air. Perhaps this insight into complicated grief can give more light to the importance of all that has been discussed so far in the many facets of the healing. "The LORD is close to the brokenhearted, / saves those whose spirit is crushed" (Ps 34:19).

Reconciling with God gives you strength and hope as you delve into each aspect of grief. This helps you to stay focused on the truth and not slip into denial. It enables you to accept God's forgiveness, and to accept yourself with compassion. Hopefully, you will experience how these pieces fit together to make the picture complete. In fact, it is God who gently puts all the pieces together in an amazing way. As you look back at your progress, may you experience awe and wonder at God's goodness. Connecting with your child on the spiritual level can close the door of fear and open the door of this positive closeness through prayer.

The most important memorial is the one in your heart, where your son or daughter lives in love. Another important memorial is the beauty of your own life that is now changing and growing through the grace of your hopeful work. Living your own life to the full is the best tribute you can give to your child. This is what your child desires for you. This is what Jesus desires for you. This gives great glory to God.

Scripture Meditations on Trust in Jesus

❖ John 11:25, 27

❖ Isaiah 30:15, 18–20

❖ Ephesians 1:17–22

❖ Mark 8:22–26

Reflection Questions

❖ Have you allowed yourself to feel the grief you have for your child and to express it in healthy ways? If so, how did you do this?

❖ What special memorial will help you to remember and honor your child?

Tips for Family Members and Friends

❖ Your loved one is now the mother of a child at peace with God. She can connect with her child through prayer. This relationship helps her to mature as a person. Her life is not defined by the abortion or any other action. Her life is defined as being a daughter of God, loved and forgiven.

❖ You, too, have a loved one entrusted to God's mercy. This child intercedes for all the family members and loved ones of the child's mother.

❖ It is important for you to grieve, too. You have lost a loved one in death.

CHAPTER 6

Forgiveness of Self

One of the scribes, when he came forward and heard them disputing and saw how well he had answered them, asked him, "Which is the first of all the commandments?" Jesus replied, "The first is this: 'Hear, O Israel! The Lord our God is Lord alone! You shall love the Lord your God with all your heart, with all your soul, with all your mind, and with all your strength.' The second is this: 'You shall love your neighbor as yourself.' There is no other commandment greater than these."

Mark 12:28–31

So far this book has had much discussion about forgiveness. Hasn't it all been covered? Not yet. The most difficult person to forgive is . . . guess who? Yourself! Why is this the most difficult task of all? You are most likely harder on yourself than you are on other people. Most of us are that way. In the passage from Mark that begins this chapter, Jesus says that the second Great Commandment is to love your neighbor *as yourself*. Think about that: not only to love your neighbor, but to love your neighbor as yourself.

That means it is important to be kind to yourself. If you don't have charity toward yourself, you are not able to be fully charitable toward your neighbor, your family, or your friends. God asks us to work on three loves: love of God, love of others, and love for ourselves. All these loves are interconnected. That is an important reason for doing the work needed to be able to give and accept forgiveness. Here is the story of an elderly woman who struggled with accepting forgiveness:

❖❖❖❖❖

Tina called the Project Rachel counseling helpline. She asked for a counselor to come visit her at her home, since she was in her mid-eighties and no longer drove a car. Tina told the counselor that after having an illegal abortion in her mid-twenties, she had carried a burden of guilt all these decades.

Tina wanted to make peace with God and with herself, realizing that her time on this earth was short. Having read about the ministry of healing after an abortion, she was hoping that it wasn't too late for her to experience healing. As Tina talked about her life, she explained that she had had an affair during her marriage when her husband was away in military service. When she realized she was pregnant, she cut off the affair and decided to get an abortion before her husband returned. Although she did not want an abortion—because she did want a child—she did not want her husband to know about the affair. A friend accompanied her for the illegal abortion.

All went well for Tina physically. However, she did have spiritual and emotional difficulties, such as struggling with anxiety and being overly protective of her subsequent children. She was always worried her husband would find out. Tina never told her husband anything and was able to keep this secret from him until he died at the age of 80. But her heart always ached for her first child; and she wondered if God had really forgiven her, even though she confessed her sin, continued going to Church, and fulfilled her obligations as a wife and mother.

Tina just could not forgive herself. What she had buried deep inside her bothered her more and more after becoming a widow. Allowing herself to finally share her story with another person gave her a certain amount of peaceful relief. She was offered additional counseling and given the names of priests she could call if she wanted to speak to one of them. The heavy burden that God never intended for her to bear for such a long time was finally lifted with the grace of God.

❦

You also have opened your heart to receive God's mercy. You have made progress in forgiving others. You understand and accept that your child forgives you, and you have again opened your heart to receive this most precious gift of acceptance from your child. How wonderful that your heart is expanding, your life is getting in balance, and you can realize the gift of peace in your entire being. These are important elements in healing your deep wound—and all of these gifts are grace from our loving Savior, Jesus Christ. Now self-forgiveness is essential for your grieving process. To complete this process, it is time to ask yourself whether you have forgiven yourself. As you grow in your understanding of the mercy and compassion of Jesus, forgiveness becomes easier.

It can help to realize that forgiveness is not a one-time event, and it might also take time for you to experience the fruit of this effort. As you did with the list of people you needed to pardon (see Chapter 4), perhaps you can make a list of specific things that you want to forgive yourself for in the abortion decision. Are you angry at yourself? Can you make a list of what you are angry about? Then reflect on each item in the light of prayer, as a step toward self-forgiveness. Ask God to help you to understand the source of your anger and to let go of this anger.

This is not a time to think badly of yourself or to be down on yourself. The purpose of this exercise is to be honest with yourself. If specific events or decisions cause you to be angry with yourself, pay attention to them. Anger is a mask. What other emotions is the anger pushing down? List these hidden emotions as you become aware of them. Don't be afraid to let them come to the surface. Maybe you discover fear, regret, or shame. Give each emotion a voice, and bring it to the light of God's love. Are you your worst enemy? Become your best friend!

Become aware of negative thoughts you may be telling yourself about yourself. Are you calling yourself negative names, such as foolish, stupid, crazy, unforgiveable? Write down these negative words. Lack of forgiveness toward yourself may be how you punish yourself. It also keeps you isolated from the people you love. It blocks you from getting to the truth. This is not healthy.

Consider how you can replace these harmful thoughts with positive thoughts about yourself. Take a "mercy moment" for yourself. Choose a merciful thought, such as "I am a child of God; God gave me a dignity that nothing can take away from me; God loves me unconditionally; God's love has changed me; I am a new creation." Make your own list of "mercy thoughts." Replace each negative thought with one of these mercy thoughts. Surrender to the grace and mercy of God. Surrender the angry memories to the Lord, so he can fill you with gentleness, patience, kindness, and peace. Have faith in God's tender care for your healing.

Perhaps you have a favorite line or phrase from one of the psalms. Write down favorite Scripture quotes or your mercy thoughts on slips of paper and put them in a small box. Each day pull one out. Then try to think of this quote or mercy thought during the day when negative thoughts come up. With time and effort, you can make this a healthy habit. This practice can draw you closer to God as you ask for his help in moments of need.

Here are some short prayers you can call to mind:

❖ Jesus, I trust in you.

❖ Lord, help me to move forward, to think of your love for me instead of focusing on my failures.

❖ Lord, help me to accept your mercy.

❖ Lord, help me to live your merciful love.

❖ Jesus, help me to begin again, to make this a new start.

❖ Jesus, please help me love myself as you love me.

❖ Thank you, God, for the gift of your mercy.

❖ Lord, help me remember that you love me.

Repeating these prayers during mercy moments really will help replace your negative thoughts with positive thoughts. Hope for a better future. Trust in God's care for your future. Take time out for mercy—mercy for your true self.

The past cannot be changed. But this is an opportunity to learn about your strengths and weaknesses. This learning can lead you to greater self-acceptance. If God has pardoned you—and he does forgive every repentant heart —then you can be merciful to yourself. Mercy and self-forgiveness lead to the only true path to move forward in your life. Be gentle with yourself.

Do you believe that you deserve this compassion and freedom? If you struggle with self-esteem, you might find this a difficult question to answer. Consider answering in a spiritual light: you are a child of God, who loves you unconditionally. Your dignity and self-worth come from this relationship. God created you out of love, and when he looks upon you, he sees your true beauty and dignity. Hopefully, as time goes on, you will find joy and new life in this knowledge—not just knowledge in your mind, but an experience of your heart. Jesus died for you to give you a totally new life. He is your Savior, your brother, your Redeemer. Let the cry of your heart be that of King David in the psalms:

> Have mercy on me, God, in accord with your
>   merciful love;
>   in your abundant compassion blot out my
>   transgressions.
> Thoroughly wash away my guilt;
>   and from my sin cleanse me.
> For I know my transgressions;
>   my sin is always before me. . . .
>
> A clean heart create for me, God;
>   renew within me a steadfast spirit.
> Do not drive me from before your face,
>   nor take from me your holy spirit.
> Restore to me the gladness of your salvation;
>   uphold me with a willing spirit. . . .
> My sacrifice, O God, is a contrite spirit;

a contrite, humbled heart, O God, you will not
scorn. (Ps 51:3–5, 12–14, 19)

Perhaps you have difficulty trusting yourself. God will
give you the strength you need to work through the challenges of the past, the present, and the future. Life is a
journey on which you continue to grow in wisdom,
knowledge, and love. Your dignity is greater and more
magnificent than any one fault, failing, or sin. Accepting
your weaknesses is also part of accepting the reality of
your humanity. No one is perfect in love. We all need other
people to support and love us. God helps you to accept
your entire self: strengths, weaknesses, gifts, and abilities.
With God to help you, you don't have to rely only on yourself. The Holy Spirit guides you in your decisions and
builds up your self-confidence. You are a beautiful daughter of God.

Consider another woman who had many gifts and was
generous to others, yet felt that part of her life was
missing:

◈⟡◈⟡◈

Susie is a married, middle-aged woman and has
four living children. She is very active at her parish
church and volunteers a lot of time in helping others. Susie describes her life as fulfilling—yet a piece

is missing. Her parents divorced when she was nine, and as a lonely teenager, she gave in to the first advance of an older boy she dated. She got pregnant, and not wanting to drop out of high school, she readily accepted her mother's suggestions of an abortion, thinking this would solve all her problems. It only made her life lonelier. Susie married in her mid-twenties and had a relatively happy and stable marriage. As her children were moving out on their own, she realized that she needed to work on healing the loss of her first child, which she had avoided for so long. Her husband, who was not the father of the child who was aborted, had been very supportive of her desire to heal.

Susie had already accepted God's forgiveness. She had more difficulty pardoning several people she believed had betrayed her during her pregnancy and subsequent abortion. Susie had a graced moment in accepting forgiveness from her child, during a special time of prayer. Yet she could not forgive herself. No matter how hard she tried, Susie was stuck in this area.

Then one day during prayer, she experienced a special visitation of Jesus. He poured his love into Susie's heart and soul by showing her his wounded hands and side. As she gazed at the marks of the Passion of Jesus, the realization that he suffered out of love for her changed her view of herself. She saw herself in the light of the love that created her and loved her into being. This pure love enabled her to experience, to the depths of her being, that she is loved with an eternal love, a love that nothing can break or stop. Susie knew in this instant that God's love is greater than anything else. Not only was she looking at Jesus, but he was looking back at her with this eternal love. This was when she received not only the gift of being restored, but the gift of new life that Jesus lovingly gave her.

❦⁓❦⁓❦

Susie's story shows that God's love is the gift that heals and brings new life. He knows the right moment when you will be able to open your heart to accept yourself as his loving child. Your task is to be willing to receive, to stay in the struggle, to be patient, and at times to wait on God. You give much of your love and time to others—now it is time for you to accept as well as to give. Saying *yes* to God's merciful love is the best act of love that you can then give to others.

Do you struggle with feeling worthy to receive God's love and pardon and to accept yourself? Make another list, this time focusing on the areas where it is hard for you to receive love. Then focus on each situation. Being specific can help you to go deeper in self-understanding. What are you telling yourself about you that keeps you from accepting the love of others?

Receiving love opens your heart to give more love to others. Your relationships can deepen and expand, including your relationship with God. Just as it is blessed to give, it is also very blessed to receive. Do you feel joyful when someone you care about is grateful for a gift you gave him or her? How much more joy you give to God when you accept his unconditional love for you!

Your dignity and worth come directly from a loving God who created you. Accepting this reality can help you to understand who you are in God and the purpose of your life. The people who love you need you—your gifts, love, talents, and all that makes you *you*! You have much to offer the world. God has created you as a unique human person to fulfill a unique mission in the world. Jesus said: "You are the light of the world. A city set on a mountain cannot be hidden. Nor do they light a lamp and then put it under a bushel basket; it is set on a lampstand, where it gives light to all in the house. Just so, your light must shine before others, that they may see your good deeds and glorify your heavenly Father" (Mt 5:14–16).

So what does healing look like and feel like? It looks like a woman who is fully alive, who radiates the peace and love of God, who is confident in who she is in God. It looks like having mature, healthy relationships with others. It means enjoying daily life and not worrying about the past or the future. Restoring your true self helps you to feel whole, with the pieces fitting together. You find new energy to invest in living life, in making plans, in fulfilling dreams, and in sleeping peacefully. You accept your strengths and weaknesses. You rely on God's love and mercy. You enjoy being with other people.

As your burdens lift, you become free to become fully that woman God created you to be. Life still brings difficulties. But now you have tools to deal confidently with life, turning to God for help. You will still grieve, especially at special anniversary dates, with thoughts like "My child would be graduating from high school today," "My child would be turning 21 today," and so on. This is normal. Now you remember your child with a special love. You have courageously faced this part of your journey, giving your hand to Jesus as he leads you to paths of joyful peace.

How very courageous you are. You are engaging in the difficult work of healing, contrition, and loving. Continue on your way, looking to Jesus to give you strength and help. Your relationship with Jesus will mature, and you will grow in holiness. The three loves mentioned at the start of this chapter will come together: love of God, love of neighbor, and love of self. The integration is ongoing and opens your heart to a greater charity that extends greater mercy to others. This brings a deeper gratitude to God for all the gifts he bestows on you, his beloved daughter. Gratitude is the wind in your sails that keeps your boat moving along.

Scripture Meditations for Restoration of Trust

◈ Revelation 3:20–21

◈ Matthew 8:23–27

◈ 1 John 4:15–19

Reflection Questions

◈ Do you experience a connection between trust and forgiveness? What is the connection?

◈ To forgive yourself, it is important to love yourself. In prayer, ask Jesus to show you how much he loves you. Open your heart to receive this love. How does it feel to receive his love?

◈ If it is difficult to forgive yourself, why? Ask Jesus to help you to accept the gift of self-forgiveness.

❖ How do you feel after someone has offered for-giveness to you? Have this same compassion for yourself.

Tip for Family Members and Friends

❖ It is usually easier to forgive others than to forgive oneself. Your loved one may struggle with self-forgiveness. Continue to be loving toward her and be patient. God is at work. Continue to encourage her and let her know if you see progress.

CHAPTER 7

The Impact of Abortion on Relationships

I pray not only for them, but also for those who will believe in me through their word, so that they may all be one, as you, Father, are in me and I in you, that they also may be in us, that the world may believe that you sent me. And I have given them the glory you gave me, so that they may be one, as we are one.

John 17:20–22

Relationships are like diamonds. The facets of a diamond show a rainbow of colors at varying depths. So too do our relationships with others have facets that reflect the beauty of each person. The human person thrives in healthy interactions and suffers in prolonged isolation or unhealthy relationships.

As an example, think about a favorite friend or relative you admire and the many dimensions of her life. She is one person with different roles based on association, such as daughter, wife, mother, aunt, friend, cousin, sister, church member, employee, leader, co-worker, and so on. Each person knows a different aspect of her life, and she influences others in unique ways. You enjoy a special facet in your own association with this person.

Healthy interactions with others are essential gifts for experiencing fulfillment in life. Growing in this area takes dedicated hard work. If you have suffered the ill effects of unhealthy relationships in the past or if you are experiencing them now, these can be healed, at best—or your internal response can at least improve, even if the other person does not change.

Unhealthy relationships in the past may have influenced your decision to have an abortion. Such associations in the present can continue to impede your healing process. Your bonds with your father and your mother powerfully shape how you perceive yourself as a parent. The way you relate to your own children can be impacted by a prior abortion. How you interact with your spouse is certainly affected, whether your abortion was before or during your marriage, whether or not your spouse is the father of the child who was aborted.

This chapter will explore each of these associations to help you find greater understanding and healing. Each of these relationships is unique. Which one is the most important to you? Which one had the most impact on you at the time of the abortion? If the missing pieces still upset you, it may be time for you to reflect on them to bring greater interior clarity.

Parents and Children

As children we learn so much from observing and imitating our parents, in both positive and negative circumstances. The involvement or absence of a parent in the household is crucial in the forming of a child. Women learn how to be mothers largely based on how their own mothers related to them. Men learn how to be fathers in the same way. If a mother or father is physically or emotionally absent from the family, this absence can have lasting negative consequences on a person's self-image and the way that person, as a parent, relates to her or his own children. Of course, the parent of the opposite sex also plays an important role in the growth and self-image of a child. If your mother was very nurturing, caring, and involved in your young life, you will most likely be the same way as a mother. If your mother was emotionally distant, ill, and unable to be an active caregiver, you may not have bonded well (attached emotionally) with her, or she might not have bonded well with you. This distance may make it more difficult for you to be emotionally close to your own children and to other people. Similarly, if one of your parents was not a good role model, was perhaps emotionally unstable, or had other difficulties, you may have doubts about your own ability to parent a child.

Early bonding through positive attachment with a parent helps a child feel safe and stable. If this does not happen, the child may become vulnerable to future abuse and possible trauma. The resulting symptoms may become part of the thoughts and behaviors that can in turn lead to depression and post-traumatic stress.[1]

On an unconscious level, a negative self-image may have influenced your decision to abort your child. Perhaps an unnamed fear held you back from accepting this child, especially if conceived in difficult circumstances. Consider a recently married couple who was

---

1. For more information about resolving trauma, see Peter A. Levine, *In an Unspoken Voice: How the Body Releases Trauma and Restores Goodness* (Berkeley: North Atlantic Books, 2010), 60.

considering an abortion because each spouse feared whether he or she could be a good parent. Fortunately, the couple discussed their fears with a spiritual advisor who helped them work through their anxieties and continue the pregnancy.

Examining some of these issues in your own life will not change past decisions; however, this process can help you to understand yourself more fully and to accept yourself in a deeper way now. Healing these wounds that influence your abilities to parent can help you to draw closer to your children now, no matter what their ages. You can also become your own self-parent by learning to trust your own wisdom and intuition.

The Impact of a Prior Abortion on Your Relationships with Children

The emotional harm from an abortion can adversely affect your ability to bond or attach emotionally to other children. This can happen if you have a child who was born before a sibling was aborted, or if you have children born afterward. This calls to mind a young client who made an appointment to see me with a presenting problem of depression:

❖❖❖❖❖

Berta was a newly arrived immigrant to this country when she found herself pregnant without any family or other resources nearby. She was too embarrassed to reach out for help from strangers in this new land. Although she wanted to keep the baby and return to her homeland, she panicked and decided to have an abortion, without giving it sufficient thought. Several years later, she had much sadness and depression, finding it difficult to function in daily life due to hypervigilance and a lack of concentration. She made an appointment to see me, stating she was depressed. Berta did not mention her abortion during the first session. She did talk about her other child, a young daughter she was raising. On her next visit, Berta mentioned, in passing, that she had a collection of brand-new baby clothes in boxes stored in the garage. Thinking this was a strange fact for her to mention, I wondered if she had lost a child in the past. Gently I worked the question of previous pregnancies into the conversation. She looked at me sadly and began to cry. Then her painful story came tumbling out between the tears.

❖❖❖❖❖

Berta may have been buying and then hiding these baby items as a way to remember her child lost to abortion, yet she was not ready to bring this part of her life into the open. We discussed her relationship with her young daughter and how important it was for her to work through the abortion of her first child, to help her find peace of mind, and to help her to be available emotionally to the child she was raising. Berta admitted that she was overprotective of her little girl, fearing something would happen to her. Unfortunately, she dropped out of counseling after a short time. Perhaps she was not yet ready to look at these issues; however, we had planted the seeds so that she could seek help in the future.

A mother may become overprotective like Berta, fearing on an unconscious level that her living child may get injured and die. In this situation, the mother might smother the child and become fearful of ordinary experiences, or may not allow the child to explore normally, which can cause the child to become inhibited emotionally. This is not good for the child, or for mother–child interactions. At the other extreme, the mother may be afraid to be emotionally close to another child, leading to attachment or bonding difficulties. For the child in this relationship, this distance can cause problems that may accompany him or her into adulthood—especially an inability to bond emotionally with others in a healthy way. Healing these difficulties brings an opportunity to break a generational cycle of attachment problems.

While a mother carries a child in her womb and decides whether or not to have an abortion, a relationship between mother and child has already begun, even if for a short time. Much goes on at a level that is not conscious. The woman may perceive the child as disruptive to her current lifestyle and relationships or might view the child as a threat to her future plans. She may be torn between wanting to be a nurturer and attach herself emotionally to the child, versus seeing the child as an intruder. This psychic conflict causes great turmoil. If the woman decides to abort her child, then she herself becomes an aggressor, a role opposed to the nurturing role that women naturally possess.

Again, your own movement toward health involves digging out weeds that can have long and destructive roots. If you think you need to examine this area in your own history, doing so can bring resolution to that psychic conflict of long ago. You may need to explore these issues with a professional counselor, especially if you feel that you are stuck at this point or feel overwhelmed with emotions.

Another difficulty that can occur when a woman is not healed from a prior abortion is an overwhelming desire to get pregnant again, to have a sort of replacement baby. This decision also does not usually happen at the conscious thought level. The unresolved emotional conflict and abrupt physical changes that result from an abortion can play havoc with hormones, feelings, and rational thinking. A woman may perceive on the unconscious level that if she gets pregnant again, it will somehow make up for the baby she aborted. But each child is unique. Another baby cannot replace the one who died. This can also cause the mother to place unrealistic expectations on the child, who may feel pressured to somehow make the mother feel better. Having another child before healing from a prior abortion does not magically make the mother's life better. In fact, it may compound the emotional and relational difficulties that are already there. There is also a risk that the mother may decide to abort the replacement baby as well, if she has not worked through the loss of the other baby. She may again give in to fears.

As you can see, the complexity of each person and each connection adds to the issues for you to address when you begin to strive for truth, peace, and inner freedom.

Spousal Relationships

Frequently the following situation occurs: a married woman has a desire to heal from a past abortion of a baby who was fathered by another man, before she met her current husband. Her husband wants to support his wife, yet he often may not know what to say to her or what to do. If you are in this situation, you may find it helpful to include your husband in the healing process. He needs to ask his questions, share his emotions, and perhaps receive some clarification on issues that may be confusing to him. This can be an opportunity for you as a couple to grow closer through honest sharing and compassion. He can give that strong, caring support that you may not have had in the past.

Some men may think, "Well, this doesn't involve me," or "Can't she just get over what happened, long before she met me?" Any life event that deeply affects one spouse can cause difficulties in the marriage if left unresolved. Hopefully your husband can understand the importance of his support and encouragement toward you. You will need to engage in your own process, yet it is so much easier when loved ones give you the space and understanding you need.

More difficult situations occur with the broken bond of trust between a husband and wife who abort their own child. This often leads to difficulties in the marital relationship, even to separation and divorce. The deepest fracture occurs in the bond of trust and unity that has now been separated from the very purpose of the marital bond—that the two become one flesh so that a child is conceived as a result of this unitive love. If one or both parents do not want the baby, in other words, the very love of this marriage breaks apart because the fruit of this love is rejected.

This destruction at such a fundamental level is rarely talked about. Distance grows between the couple due to unspoken anger, mistrust, depression, or lowered self-esteem of either the husband or the wife. Too many people walk away from each other because they are not ready to look at their role in the decision to abort. Much of this knowledge lies at a psychological and spiritual depth that requires great openness in discussion. Due to the intensity of emotion and the shattering of the relationship, this level of vulnerability may not be possible in a marital relationship shortly after the abortion. Each spouse may withdraw into his or her own shell and never bridge the distance.

Men and women grieve differently. This can also cause communication problems. Men may bury their sorrow in work, sports, or even addictions. They may be reluctant to talk about their grief. Women often find it more healing to express their thoughts and feelings.

This very deep wound occurring from such a break in trust and the unity of the marital bond is difficult to heal. Yet if you are in this situation, please know that it is possible to reach this goal, with God's help. Couples have achieved this reconciliation, though it takes struggle and hard work in communicating and regaining trust. I am reminded of one couple who struggled greatly with this issue:

❖⤙❖⤙❖

Annalea was a very gentle woman who had worked hard in her career. She and her husband had been married for seven years and although they wanted children, Annalea had not been able to conceive. They decided to go to a doctor for help. Annalea did conceive and all was well for a few months. Then her first ultrasound revealed that the child had genetic abnormalities. Further testing was done. The doctors presented the situation in such dire terms that the couple panicked. The doctors pressured Annalea and her husband to have an abortion, stating how hard it would be for them to care for this child, how much the child would suffer, and so on. The doctors said the couple would have to decide within one week. Even though several people encouraged them to take their time, see another doctor, and work with a perinatal hospice, Annalea and her husband were so frightened they would not listen. They did not know that there are couples willing to adopt babies with abnormalities. Although Annalea and her husband wanted this baby, they gave in to the pressure and fears and rushed into the decision to abort the baby.

Within a few months, their marriage began to suffer. Her husband had his own guilt, feeling he had failed to protect his wife and his child. Annalea doubted her ability to be a nurturer. Anger led them to argue about things they had never fought about before the abortion. They didn't talk about how the abortion affected them. They silently blamed each other for the decision to abort. Finally, Annalea decided to talk to someone about this anxiety and guilt. After a few sessions, she agreed that her husband should attend the sessions, too. The journey was a rough one, because the bond of trust had been fractured in their marriage. Annalea looked to her spouse as the protector of herself and their child and felt that he had failed to welcome this child into their lives. Annalea also felt she had failed in her role as a mother.

Together, they were able to gradually express the deep feelings of mistrust and guilt. Their love was strong, and they were able to experience personal healing and strengthening in their marital relationship. But this healing took much time and hard work. They were a fortunate couple. A high percentage of couples, even married couples, break apart after an abortion.[2]

❖❖❖❖❖

When one spouse wants an abortion and the other doesn't, the marriage can greatly suffer. If a wife has an abortion and tells her husband after the fact, and he wanted the child, the betrayal is devastating. If a husband pressures his wife to have an abortion, and she really doesn't want to do so but gives in to his pressure, she may be very resentful. Unless each spouse is willing to face the truth of the abortion decision and work to heal the rifts it

---

2. For more on how couples can break apart after abortion, see Priscilla K. Coleman, "The Decline of Partner Relationships in the Aftermath of Abortion," *Association for Interdisciplinary Research in Values and Social Change Research Bulletin* 20, no. 1 (Winter 2007), http://rupetacerea.ro/wp-content/uploads/2012/05/The-Decline-of-Partner-Relationships-in-the-Aftermath-of-Abortion.pdf.

created, the gulf becomes too wide. This is a very tragic situation.

Lack of communication, different ways of grieving, and feelings of guilt, anger, and depression can lead to emotional isolation, sexual difficulties, and other communication problems. The wife suffers, the husband suffers, the couple suffers, the marriage suffers.[3]

The same issues occur in relationships between girl friends and boyfriends. Lack of commitment followed by betrayal can have a huge effect on the relationship, which usually leads to a breakup. This presents a sad irony. A woman may agree to an abortion in hopes of keeping the relationship together, but the decision to reject the baby leads to breakup nonetheless.

Relatives

Relatives may also grieve the loss of a family member when they find out about the abortion. Perhaps they grieve in painful silence. Hopefully, they can talk to someone who can help them mourn this loss. American Victims of Abortion and other associations listed in Appendix 3 can

---

3. See Coleman, "Decline of Partner Relationships."

be useful resources in these areas. Family relationships become even more difficult if the woman who had the abortion has not disclosed this to a family member, who then found out through some other means. The family member can get help for himself or herself and must respect whether the woman is ready to disclose her story.

You may find that telling other people about your abortion depends on their need to know and your own readiness to share. You are the only one who can decide this and set the conditions and boundaries for disclosure to others. You have no obligation to tell your sins to anyone outside of the Sacrament of Reconciliation. You must find a balance between healthy sharing versus sharing with too many people versus keeping a secret that can be destructive. In our society, it is a common practice to "tell all," as we see on reality TV shows with thousands of viewers. But the popularity of the practice does not mean that this is a healthy thing to do.

It would be harmful for your loved ones to find out about your abortion through a stranger or through an impersonal public disclosure. Discernment and prudence help you move closer toward emotional and spiritual health. You also want to protect yourself. Premature disclosure may expose you to an internal emotional reaction that you are not strong enough to handle. This experience could set back your healing process. You may want to consult a certified trauma therapist who is grounded in Christian values to discuss the important matter of when and how to disclose the information, and to whom.

Advanced studies of how trauma affects the brain and central nervous system have led psychologists and psychiatrists to affirm this best practice of not discussing traumatic events in detail. Healing can occur without revisiting these trigger points. Dr. Peter Levine offers this caution: "Some cathartic methods that encourage intense emotional reliving of trauma may be harmful. I believe that in the long run, cathartic approaches create a dependency on continuing catharsis. . . . Because of the nature of trauma, there is a good chance that the cathartic reliving of an experience can be traumatizing rather than healing."[4] The goal is to be relieved of the negative psychological distress, not to add to it. Van der Kolk agrees: "If elements of the trauma are replayed again and again, the accompanying stress hormones engrave those memories ever more deeply in the mind. Ordinary, day-to-day events become less and less compelling."[5] If people ask you to

---

4. Peter A. Levine, *Waking the Tiger: Healing Trauma* (Berkeley: North Atlantic Books, 1997), 10.

5. Van der Kolk, *The Body Keeps the Score*, 67.

share such details and you are not ready, stand your ground. Take care to not retraumatize yourself. Being in control of your decisions leads to greater hope and self-determination. Set a healthy boundary by asking loved ones to support you with love and to respect your decisions regarding disclosure.

It is especially important to discern whether to tell your own children about your abortion. If you decide to disclose your experiences to them, they need to be mature enough not to be overwhelmed by this information. They should be at an age where they can understand the information and have the emotional ability to integrate this information into their own lives. If you choose to disclose, be sure it is because you are healed enough to handle this disclosure and can do it freely, not out of compulsion or guilt. You have no obligation to tell them. It is important to discern whether the relationship with your children is strong enough for you to work through issues together that will arise with the disclosure. Discussing this with a person you trust and praying for guidance are essential in coming to a decision.

Disclosing a prior abortion to a spouse who was not the father of the aborted baby is another serious consideration. Think about your reasons for disclosing or not. Keeping important secrets from a spouse can erode trust and communications. The ideal time for you to disclose this history is before your marriage. If yours is a strong relationship based on true love, it will flourish. If the revelation causes difficulties before the marriage, then this is the best time to work on resolving the difficulties, before making a lifetime commitment. Consulting an advisor in this matter can be helpful.

Relationships are gifts that make life full and meaningful. They are ways to give and receive love, and they help you mature in your relationship with God. As with other issues in life, they involve hard work. Be not afraid—Jesus is with you, ready to help you. "The one who supplies seed to the sower and bread for food will supply and multiply your seed and increase the harvest of your righteousness" (2 Cor 9:10).

Perhaps you feel as though your life is like a clear image in a mirror that has become distorted, leaving a fuzzy view. The good news is that Jesus helps you to see the pure image without any distortions: "He will wipe every tear from their eyes, and there shall be no more death or mourning, wailing or pain, [for] the old order has passed away. The one who sat on the throne said, 'Behold, I make all things new'" (Rev 21:4–5).

As you grow to see your true self in the light of the face of Jesus, you also radiate his light. The glimpse of Jesus' face gives you the victory, because you now know who you truly are. Jesus said to his disciples: "Amen, amen, I say to you, you will weep and mourn, while the world rejoices; you will grieve, but your grief will become joy. . . . So you also are now in anguish. But I will see you again, and your hearts will rejoice, and no one will take your joy away from you" (Jn 16:20, 22).

Scripture Meditations for Healing of Relationships

- ◆ Hebrews 10:19–25
- ◆ Luke 5:17–20
- ◆ John 15:9–17

Reflection Questions

- ◆ Are your relationships satisfying and enriching? If yes, what elements make it so? If not, what elements are lacking?

- ◆ With whom do you wish you had a closer relationship? Why? What would help you to grow closer?

- ◆ If you did not receive adequate parenting as a child, you can parent yourself to grow in emotional maturity. Do you trust your own wisdom and intuition?

❖ If you are married, and you and your spouse agreed to an abortion, are you willing to work together in counseling to help heal the difficulties caused by this decision?

Tips for Family Members and Friends

❖ Perhaps your loved one has isolated herself from you and others. Shame and low self-esteem may weigh her down. Depression or other ill effects may keep her at an emotional distance. Be constant in your love and attention. Invite her to participate in social events, but don't be forceful. Try not to insist that she share details of her pain with you.

❖ Help your loved one to find joy in life.

❖ Take time to listen and show you care.

❖ If you are the husband of a woman who had an abortion before you met her, you can be a source of healing by being a patient listener, showing her constant love and support. She needs to know that you value her as a person of worth and dignity.

CHAPTER 8

How Abortion Affects Men

Put on then, as God's chosen ones, holy and beloved, heartfelt compassion, kindness, humility, gentleness, and patience, bearing with one another and forgiving one another, if one has a grievance against another; as the Lord has forgiven you, so must you also do. And over all these put on love, that is, the bond of perfection. And let the peace of Christ control your hearts, the peace into which you were also called in one body. And be thankful.

Colossians 3:12–15

Most people seeking healing after an abortion are women. However, many men can also suffer aftereffects that seriously impact their lives. They usually deal with this in ways that are very different from how women cope. Highlighting some of these differences can help develop a better understanding and, hopefully, better communication that can lead to forgiveness and wholeness.

Men often have been socialized to keep their feelings to themselves and not to express emotions in public. From an early age, many boys are taught in their families and from cultural norms that they must not cry and should not express sadness, fear, or loss to anyone. As adults, they often do not confide these feelings to male friends, or even acknowledge these feelings to themselves. Men tend to process information and events by mentally compartmentalizing the various aspects of their lives.

Thus most men repress an abortion event in one compartment in their mind and suffer in silence. This repression can lead to possible harmful effects such as post-traumatic stress, depression, addictions, risky behaviors, sexual addictions, and even thoughts of suicide. The symptoms of post-traumatic stress can arise from hearing about the abortion of the child or by sitting in the waiting room of the abortion facility. The man knows that the life of his own child is being taken, even if he blocks out those thoughts at the time. According to Levine, "Chronically traumatized individuals go through the motions of living without really feeling vital or engaged in life. . . . Chronic immobility gives rise to the core emotional symptoms of trauma: numbness, shutdown, entrapment, helplessness, depression, fear, terror, rage and hopelessness."[1] A man in this situation might need help to grieve and to work through this loss so that he can fully engage in his life and be fully present in the relationships that are important to him.

Since the Supreme Court legalized abortion in its 1973 *Roe v. Wade* decision, men have had no legal rights to protect the life of their child in the womb. Legally, the decision to procure an abortion is totally up to the mother. The father of the child is powerless to stop the abortion to save the life of the child. This adds a dimension of suffering—even rage—for the man who does not want the abortion to occur.

Men are involved in the abortion decision in various ways. Some men may pressure the mother of the child to have the abortion, while others may be ambivalent or run away. Some men do not know about the pregnancy or subsequent abortion until afterward. Some may try to stop the abortion or offer alternatives to the woman. Each of these different situations has an impact on a man whose

---

1. Levine, *In an Unspoken Voice*, 67.

child is aborted. According to Dr. E. Joanne Angelo, men who do not want the abortion and try to stop it often feel impacted by the lack of legal rights granted to them. They may feel powerless and helpless in their natural desires to protect and save. Men who want the abortion or pressure a woman to have an abortion, or those who stand on the sidelines, may later experience strong self-doubt and guilt. Regardless of the original circumstances, these men can become very angry, experience the reality of broken trust, and suffer effects of trauma such as numbing of emotions and anxiety.[2]

Men and women grieve differently. Some men struggle with feelings of low self-esteem, believing they betrayed their duty as protectors and leaders. Because many men are socialized not to express emotion to others, they often grieve in silence, whereas women may be more willing to express their feelings. Yet with all these differences, men still need to grieve losses, heal the inner brokenness, forgive, and find wholeness. Men are hardwired to be protectors of women in their lives and to provide for the well-being of their children. Being involved in an abortion

---

2. E. Joanne Angelo, "Portraits of Grief in the Aftermath of Abortion," Hope After Abortion, August 8, 2011, http://hopeafterabortion.com/?page=106.

can make it difficult for men to experience healthy relationships in the future.

This buried emotional pain can immobilize the emotional life of a man and keep him stuck. Any threat to his child normally sets a man in motion to prevent harm. In the language of trauma, it sets him physiologically into fight mode. The reality that he cannot or does not act on this threat leaves him stuck in this uncompleted set of actions, both physically and emotionally. This can in turn lead to unresolved aggression, grief, and feelings of failure. Seeking help from a therapist who specializes in trauma therapy can help a man in this situation to resolve this hidden distress through specialized activities that help the body reset those incomplete actions to protect and save. "Trauma represents a profound compression of 'survival' energy, energy that has not been able to complete its meaningful course of action."[3]

Men who either let the woman decide on the abortion or are ambivalent about it can suffer from confusion about their part in the actual abortion. Dr. Catherine Coyle explains the effects on men in a study she conducted:

> Role confusion was expressed as a direct result of the seemingly contradictory demands of a society that

---

3. Levine, *In an Unspoken Voice*, 349.

wants men to care for and support their offspring but simultaneously denies them the ability to care for their children before birth. A majority of men also discussed their perceived need to put aside their own discomfort as they attempted to support their partners. . . . Thus, many men are prone to passively accept a woman's suggestion that she have an abortion. Since he feels his role is to suppress his own emotions and as she has the legal right to obtain abortion, he is not likely to debate the abortion decision with his partner. Unfortunately, then, he is also not likely to have the kind of discussion with his partner that would lead her to keep their child.[4]

Unfortunately, some men turn to addictions such as alcohol, drugs, sex, and overwork to numb the inner distress. Obviously, this only worsens the situation. Men may need help to experience and understand their emotions and begin to put words to these feelings. Often men are reluctant to seek professional help, due to socialization that implies men should "grin and bear it." When their lives begin to fall apart, or marital problems arise, men may be pressed to seek help. They might seek counseling for crisis issues; and after some time, they might reveal an

---

4. Catherine Coyle, "An Online Pilot Study to Investigate the Effects of Abortion on Men," (Winter, 2006), http://www.lifeissues.net/writers/air/air_vol19no1_2006.html.

abortion in their history that is causing unresolved grief and pain, adversely affecting present relationships and peace of mind.

❖❀❖❀❖

Larry was emotionally disconnected from his girlfriend, Meg. He had a charismatic personality and was always joking. People were attracted to him because of his carefree attitude. Larry's father had been in and out of his life, never there when Larry needed his guidance. Larry drifted in and out of relationships. Although he was strongly attracted to Meg, it was hard for Larry to make a commitment. When he found out that she was pregnant and wanted to get married, Larry was not ready to make that permanent commitment and to be a father. Instead of talking to Meg about how to provide for this child and for her, Larry only offered abortion as a solution. He did not want to be tied down. Meg was confused herself and looked to Larry for strength and guidance. His reaction was not the response she wanted, but she went along with it. Larry was uneasy after driving Meg home from the abortion, although he did not dwell on this. He began drinking more than usual and became even more emotionally distant.

His relationship with Meg ended. Larry felt he was even more inadequate, that he was more like his absent father than he wanted to admit. Running away from his true self, he became addicted to alcohol and to short-term relationships. It was only when he hit rock bottom that Larry sought help. Through counseling, he discovered that the abortion of his child was at the root of these addictive behaviors.

❖◞❀◟❀◞❖

As previous chapters have explained, working to restore integrity through forgiveness is crucial. This involves forgiving oneself and others, as well as accepting forgiveness from God. To work through feelings of anger and rage, men may experience calm by doing physical work such as manual labor or building projects, working out at the gym, or engaging in other types of physical activities. This type of concrete action can be more effective to help men work out their emotions. Men also may relate better when focusing on their thoughts, as opposed to their feelings, at least in the initial stages of healing.

Exploring key relationships in early life is important. Because recent generations have had a higher percentage of single-parent families, many boys are raised without a father or father figure. Without a male role model, they may experience much confusion as to what is important as they mature into manhood. As adults, men can learn to be protectors and providers even if they did not have helpful male role models as children. They can learn how to experience healthy relationships. If a man did not know his father growing up, and then he later cooperates with his girlfriend or wife in procuring an abortion, he may do so out of an unspoken fear of not knowing how to be an effective father himself. The abortion may also shatter his dreams of marriage and family, at least until he works on healing these losses. He might grieve this lost fatherhood, feeling the loss of playing ball with his child, the loss of being a coach on his child's sports team, and sharing other events. An abortion during marriage is even more devastating, as it breaks the bonds of trust and intimacy inherent in the marriage vows. (See Chapter 7 for more information on the effects of abortion on relationships.)

When a couple does not talk about the consequences an abortion has had on their relationship, they are likely headed toward a breakup. The reality that men and women experience and process the aftereffects of abortion in different ways makes it crucial for them to express their confusion, hurt, anger, and other feelings to each other. It is also important that each patiently listen to and seek to understand each other. Here is one couple's story:

❖

Michael and Lidia had been married for nine years and had two children. Michael's job was on shaky ground, as his company had taken some severe financial losses in the last two years. He was afraid of being laid off. When Lidia told him she was pregnant, he got very angry. This was one more stress that he didn't want to deal with. They were barely able to pay the bills as things were. Michael told Lidia this was not a good time for another child in the family. She was devastated. Lidia loved her children and was so happy to be pregnant again. Michael continued to vacillate between anger and silence toward his wife. Lidia was worn down by his behavior and concerned about the family dynamics. She eventually agreed to the abortion, very reluctantly.

Afterward, Lidia became very depressed and withdrawn. Michael did not want to discuss the abortion, and he could not understand why Lidia was so depressed. He would say, "Just get on with life." He attempted to carry on as before, yet they grew apart from one another. There was no communication, no attempt to understand what each one was going through, and seemingly no way to resolve this breach. They did eventually agree to go to marriage counseling; and through much struggle and hard work, they began to express the loss, grief, and anger they felt toward each other. Their marriage had a strong foundation that helped them to forgive each other and to go forward. Their communication improved, helping them continue the work of healing that will go on throughout their marriage. They await the day when they will be reunited with their child in Heaven.

❖~❖~❖

See Chapter 7 for suggestions for a husband whose wife had an abortion before meeting him. More resources exist now for men seeking to heal from abortion (see Appendix 3), yet they are not reaching many men who need them. Men who have been healed could do more to reach out to other men through a peer ministry in which they offer support and encouragement. The community aspect of healing helps men to integrate their past and fully engage in the present moment. It is essential that men heal from the devastating effects of abortion—for their own peace of mind and for mending relationships and families. Trust in the healing power of God and the hope for new life through the Resurrection of Jesus Christ.

Scripture Meditations for Repentance

- ❖ Psalm 51
- ❖ Matthew 9:9–13
- ❖ Luke 15:11–32

Reflection Questions

- ❖ Has someone in your life hurt you deeply? Forgiveness may be difficult, but it can bring freedom to you. Make a list of what you are angry about, and ask God to help you pardon this person.

- ❖ Effective communication is a two-way journey. How can you improve your own communication skills?

Tips for Family Members and Friends

- ❖ If a male family member or friend discloses an abortion in his history, listen to him with compassion and patience, not judgment. Accept him as a person who needs healing and mercy. Encourage him to get professional help if an addiction is interfering with his daily living.

- ❖ See the Appendix 3 for online resources to help men seeking peace after an abortion.

❖ It is important for both women and men who want healing to learn more about the differences in the ways men and women process information, communicate, grieve, and resolve issues. Greater understanding of these differences is crucial to heal relationships.

CHAPTER 9

Live Your Life in Peace

Peace I leave with you; my peace I give to you. Not as the world gives do I give it to you. Do not let your hearts be troubled or afraid.

John 14:27

Every day is a new day. Each day God continues to heal you, in ways that you may not even be aware of. Hopefully, your life continues to be full of joy and hope, even in the midst of daily struggles and challenges. Your deeper relationship with Christ helps you to cope with all the unexpected ups and downs of life. You are freer to give your love and talents to enrich the lives of others. "I am confident of this, that the one who began a good work in you will continue to complete it until the day of Christ Jesus" (Phil 1:6).

It is very important to focus on your main vocation in life. If you are married, give the best of yourself to your husband and children, and to your extended family. Be a giver of life in all the little and great ways that can make others happy. If you are single, be attentive to your family and friends. Making time to help others is a great gift to them. Show to others—family, friends, fellow churchgoers, co-workers—the joy and peace that Christ has blessed you with. This is a tremendous witness to the gift of life. Joy attracts others to Christ.

Stay close to Jesus by praying and receiving the sacraments. Just as a relationship with a loved one or a friend needs to be nourished with regular contact and sharing, the same is true of being a child of God. Jesus is always waiting for a loving glance or a prayer from you. The psalmist says: "One thing I ask of the Lord; / this I seek: / To dwell in the Lord's house / all the days of my life, / To gaze on the Lord's beauty, / to visit his temple" (Ps 27:4).

Studying Pope Saint John Paul II's work on the Theology of the Body can help you to have a deeper understanding of God's original plan of salvation for the human person. This integration of the person, the beauty of all the gifts given, can give you a fresh experience of a life of grace. His work was intended to help everyone, not just married people. Many books are available that can help make the Theology of the Body easy to understand.

Think of the story of the woman who suffered with a hemorrhage for twelve years (see Luke 8:43–48). Usually, we do not touch a stranger, and this was even more the case in ancient Israel. Not wanting to make a scene, the woman touched only the tassel of Jesus' garment. This woman must have seen him at a distance and experienced his peace in a way that gave her confidence. Even so, touching his garment in front of a crowd required a great act of courage. And Jesus gave her complete healing because of her faith. You can approach Jesus in the same way, with confidence that he will hear you and will respond to your request. Words are not always necessary, for the Lord knows what is in your heart. Just look at him with love, gaze into his face, and experience the return of that everlasting love. As you grow in this sharing with Jesus, you will learn the depths of his care and concern for you.

As a person grows closer to Jesus, the desire to help others increases. Prayer often leads to acts of kindness to others. Perhaps you are considering ways to volunteer your time to help other people. This very generous desire comes from deep within your compassionate heart. But careful discernment in this area is important. You have a primary obligation to take care of yourself and your family members before reaching out to others. To be free interiorly to be available to others, you must be at peace and comfortable with the service you choose to do, and be sure that you are offering your time for positive reasons. God knows you will be more effective if you are free to love and give of yourself.

But not everyone desires to volunteer. That is fine. Your primary relationships and responsibilities are the most important work for you. Out of a great desire to help others, women can get overinvolved, and then care of family and oneself suffers. A balance is always important. Prudence calls for you to focus on primary responsibilities first.

The opportunities to give others your time and energy are open-ended and ever-present. For example, tutoring a child who is unable to read gives that child the gift of confidence and self-empowerment and increases his or her opportunities for a fuller life. Visiting an elderly person in a nursing home gives hope to someone who may be very lonely. There are so many ways you can bring the love of Christ to others. Pray about where your interests and talents are, and ask Christ to show you where you can serve him. Service to others is a two-way street: in giving to others, you will also receive.

The Corporal Works of Mercy are tangible ways to serve Jesus by serving others: to feed the hungry, to give drink to the thirsty, to clothe the naked, to shelter the homeless, to visit the sick, to visit the imprisoned, and to bury the dead. The Spiritual Works of Mercy are also very important: to counsel the doubtful, to instruct the uninformed, to admonish the sinner, to comfort the sorrowful, to forgive injuries, to bear wrongs patiently, and to pray for the living and the dead.

Because of your own experiences and the healing love with which Christ has blessed you, you may be a source of hope, comfort, and encouragement for others in difficult situations. You can share how the Lord has helped you (even without disclosing your own abortion, if you choose to keep that private). You can also speak your wisdom, be patient with others, and forgive them. All these acts of mercy help you to grow in holiness and to spread the Good News of the Gospel. You can pray for others in any place and at any time.

Remember what Pope Saint John Paul II wrote: "With the friendly and expert help and advice of other people, and as a result of your own painful experience, you can be among the most eloquent defenders of everyone's right to life. Through your commitment to life, whether by accepting the birth of other children or *by welcoming and caring for those most in need of someone to be close to them, you will become promoters of a new way of looking at human life."*[1] (Emphasis mine.)

What a joyful commission you have been given!

Healing from the loss of your child is a lifetime journey. As the painful memories fade and are replaced with the fullness that comes with healing, you may still experience times of loss. Anniversary dates surrounding your child might bring up old, painful thoughts and feelings. This is normal. Remember to acknowledge this, lift it up to the Lord in prayer, and ask Jesus to help you in this moment of sorrow. Here is a beautiful testimony to new life and ongoing blessings from another woman whose life has been changed by the healing of Jesus:

> I was so thankful to Jesus, and still am thankful to Jesus today as I reflect on these moments in my healing journey. There is so much *joy* and gratitude in my heart to Jesus, and always to the support companion he chose for me. I am convinced that I received a miracle . . . actually, many miracles, in my healing journey. Reflecting on this always makes me smile because it reminds me that the healing journey never ends, not until I see Jesus face to face.

---

1. John Paul II, *Evangelium*, no. 99.

If you get stuck, people are ready to listen to you and help you over this rough spot. You have learned so many ways to cope with negative thoughts and feelings and to return to a peaceful heart. Continue to practice these skills that are helpful for you. Take care of these feelings as they arise; don't let them turn into stubborn weeds that are hard to remove. You may find you need more support from time to time. It is healthy to seek out counsel again if you find it necessary.

Be at peace. Find people who give life and energy to you, and spend time with them. Be part of the community of believers who uphold one another in prayer and fellowship. Cultivate the relationships that are meaningful to you. Be humble enough to ask for help when you need it.

My constant prayer for you is that Jesus will give you all the peace, joy, and other blessings that you need and desire. Be of great courage. You are part of the Body of Christ. You are a child of God. Remember that God always sees your true beauty and goodness. I pray that you see yourself in the same way.

> The LORD bless you and keep you!
> The LORD let his face shine upon you, and be gracious
> to you!
> The LORD look upon you kindly and give you peace!
> (Nm 6:24–26)

Scripture Meditations for Growth in Your New Life

◈ Ephesians 3:14–20

◈ Hebrews 12:1–3

◈ John 15:1–8

Reflection Questions

◈ How do you enrich your relationship with God each day? Focus on what is most helpful for you. Be attentive and active in this relationship. Just as in our human relationships, a connection with God must be cultivated.

◈ What have you learned by reading this book? What is helpful to you? Continue to pray, read Scripture, worship God on Sundays, and use the skills to help you cope in daily life.

◈ What areas do you think you need to continue to focus on? Make a list. Be attentive to this. The healing continues daily.

◈ Pray for respect for all human life and for healing for others. Your prayers are powerful and help more than you can imagine.

Tips for Family Members and Friends

❖ Encourage your loved one to share her gifts and talents in ways that bring new life to your loved one, as she gives to others.

❖ Some women become involved in pro-life activities before they are healed enough to do so. Encourage your loved one to seek counsel in the best way to help others.

❖ Not everyone wants to volunteer. Praying for others is powerful, as well as being attentive to primary relationships and duties.

Acknowledgments

My deep thanks to all who encouraged the writing of this book, to those who prayed for the writer, and to all who will read it. Special thanks go to my dear friend Debbie, whose support got me started on this book and kept me going forward; my friends and mentors, Rachel and Olivia, who shared their wisdom and knowledge over the years; Father Tom, the first editor of the manuscript; my sisters in community who gave me spiritual support; several women who shared their own reflections to be included in the text; and so many others who gave support throughout. Thanks also to those who encouraged me initially to respond to the call to proceed into this ministry, Sister Brigid and Sister Patricia M. Also I send my gratitude to the Daughters of St. Paul, for working with me on the publication of this book. May God be praised.

APPENDIX 1

How to Look Up Passages in the Bible

You can find Scripture texts in books or online. The United States Conference of Catholic Bishops hosts the New American Bible, Revised Edition, at www.usccb. org/bible/books-of-the-bible. The list of the books is on one page; just click on the book and chapter that you want to read. Other versions of the Bible are also online.

In the printed Bible, it is easier to look up a Scripture passage if you have Bible tabs at the beginning of each book. In the front of your Bible you can find a list of the books and their abbreviations. For example, to look up Luke 6:36–38, go to the Gospel of Luke, then find chapter 6, and then look for verses 36 to 38. Footnotes explain some of the passages and give references to similar passages in other books of the Bible. You can view a YouTube video to assist you: www. youtube.com/watch?v=8fKbtabAIqk.

Appendix 2

How to Pray with the Bible

You can read the Bible like any other book. It is important to read it slowly and to pause for prayer if a
passage really speaks to your heart. The Bible is the living
Word of God. The Holy Spirit is always speaking through
this written word. You may be amazed to find that you can
read the same passage many times and receive a new
inspiration each time.

One way to pray with Scripture has been practiced
since the early days of Christianity: the *lectio divina,* which
literally means "holy reading." *Lectio divina* has six main
steps:

1. Pray to the Holy Spirit.

2. *Lectio:* Read the Scripture text.

3. *Meditatio:* Meditate or reflect on the text.

4. *Oratio:* Pray with the text.

5. *Contemplatio:* Contemplate or rest in God's word.

6. Pray with the text.

Let's look at these in greater detail.

The first step is to *pray to the Holy Spirit.* You might use a prayer from a prayer book, or you can simply use your own words to ask the Holy Spirit to be with you and help you understand God's Word.

The next step is to *read the text.* Read it slowly, once or twice, maybe even aloud. Ask yourself, what is happening in the text? Ask yourself questions about it. For example, if you are reading a Gospel passage, you could ask how Jesus might look and sound.

Next, *reflect.* Go a little bit deeper. Ask yourself not just what the text is saying, but what it is saying to *you.* What does God desire to tell you? How is he inviting you to grow or change?

Then *rest in the Word that God has spoken to you.* It can help to think of a short prayer or a phrase from the Scripture passage that can accompany you throughout your day.

The sixth step is to *pray.* God has offered you an invitation—how will you respond? You can pray for the grace to recognize the presence of Jesus throughout the day. You can tell Jesus that his invitation makes you feel happy, but a little frightened at the same time. During this prayer, enter into conversation with God. He speaks to you through his Word, and he wants to hear what you have to say.

Finally, end your *lectio divina* by praying in thanksgiving for God's Word. Ask him for the grace and strength to live his invitation to you.

Appendix 3

Web and Print Resources

A word of caution: Abortion providers have their own "healing" websites, which do not acknowledge the truth about abortion or its harmful effects. Read carefully when you search the Web on your own. The resources listed here provide reliable help for those seeking healing consistent with the teachings of the Catholic Church.

Finding a Catholic Therapist

- ◈ Catholic Therapists: www.catholictherapists.com
- ◈ Catholic Psychotherapy Association: www.catholic psychotherapy.org

Healing After Abortion

- ◈ Bethesda—The House of Mercy: www.bethesda houseofmercy.org

- ❖ Entering Canaan: enteringcanaan.com
- ❖ National Office of Post-Abortion Reconciliation & Healing: www.noparh.org
- ❖ Project Rachel Ministry (official Catholic diocesan-based ministry in the U.S.): hopeafterabortion.org
- ❖ Project Rachel in Canada:
      projectrachel.ca
      campaignlifecoalition.com/healing-centers
      www.no parh.org/ProjectRachels_international
- ❖ Respect Life/Family Life office of your local Catholic diocese

Healing for Men

- ❖ Entering Canaan: enteringcanaan.com
- ❖ Gregory Hasek, MA/MFT: www.swflchristian counseling.org
- ❖ Project Joseph, Kansas City: www.projectrachelkc. com/help-for-men
- ❖ Project Joseph, Dallas: projectjosephdallas.org
- ❖ Reclaiming Fatherhood: www.menandabortion. info

Perinatal Hospice for Babies with Adverse Prenatal Diagnosis

❖ Archdiocese of Baltimore's Respect Life Office: www.archbalt.org/respect-life/adverse-prenatal-diagnosis-disabilities

❖ Be Not Afraid: www.benotafraid.net/about-us

❖ Isaiah's Promise: www.isaiahspromise.net

❖ Perinatal Hospice and Pallative Care: www.perinatalhospice.org

❖ Prenatal Partners for Life: www.prenatalpartnersforlife.org

Adoption Services for Babies with Adverse Prenatal Diagnoses

❖ Reece's Rainbow Special Needs Adoption Support: reecesrainbow.org

Memorial Gardens for Mothers and Babies

❖ National Memorial for the Unborn: www.memorialfortheunborn.org

❖ National Shrine of the Divine Mercy: memorialsonedenhill.org/sothi

❖ Sacramento Memorial Garden: www.sacunbornmemorial.org

Family Members

❖ American Victims of Abortion, National Right to Life: www.nrlc.org/outreach/ava

❖ Entering Canaan: enteringcanaan.com/siblings

General Pro-Life Resources

❖ American Association of Pro-Life Obstetricians & Gynecologists: www.AAPLOG.org

❖ Divine Mercy Care: www.divinemercycare.org

❖ Heartbeat International/CareNet Pregnancy Centers: www.HeartbeatInternational.org and www.Care-Net.org

❖ NaProTechnology (fertility and natural family planning): www.naprotechnology.com

❖ National Right to Life: www.nrlc.org

❖ Pregnancy Centers in USA: optionline.org

❖ Tepeyac OB/BYN: www.tepeyacobgyn.com

❖ Theology of the Body Institute: tobinstitute.org

❖ United States Conference of Catholic Bishops: www.usccb.org/prolife

Information on Addiction Recovery

❖ Catholic in Recovery: catholicinrecovery.com

❖ RECLAIM Plan for Sexual Health: reclaimsexual
health.com

Research on Abortion and Aftereffects

❖ American Association of Therapists Treating
Abortion Related Trauma: www.abortiontrauma
treatment.org

❖ Breast Cancer Prevention Institute: www.bcpinsti
tute.org

❖ Elliot Institute: www.afterabortion.org

❖ World Expert Consortium for Abortion Research
and Education (WeCare): wecareexperts.org

Books on Related Topics

Curley, Marie Paul. *See Yourself Through God's Eyes: 52
Meditations to Grow in Self-Esteem.* Boston: Pauline
Books & Media, 2009.

Dimech-Juchniewicz, Jean. *Facing Infertility: A Catholic
Approach.* Boston: Pauline Books & Media, 2012.

Hermes, Kathryn J. *Reclaim Regret: How God Heals Life's
Disappointments.* Boston: Pauline Books & Media,
2018.

————. *Surviving Depression: A Catholic Approach.* Boston: Pauline Books & Media, 2012.

Lejeune, Marcel. *Cleansed: A Catholic Guide to Freedom From Porn.* Boston: Pauline Books & Media, 2016.

Percy, Anthony. *The Theology of the Body Made Simple.* Boston: Pauline Books & Media, 2005

BOOKS & MEDIA

A mission of the Daughters of St. Paul

As apostles of Jesus Christ, evangelizing today's world:

We are CALLED to holiness
by God's living Word and Eucharist.

We COMMUNICATE the Gospel message
through our lives and through all
available forms of media.

We SERVE the Church
by responding to the hopes and needs
of all people with the Word of God,
in the spirit of St. Paul.

For more information visit us at www.pauline.org.

BOOKS & MEDIA

The Daughters of St. Paul operate book and media centers at the following addresses. Visit, call, or write the one nearest you today, or find us at www.paulinestore.org.

CALIFORNIA
3908 Sepulveda Blvd, Culver City, CA 90230   310-397-8676
3250 Middlefield Road, Menlo Park, CA 94025   650-562-7060

FLORIDA
145 S.W. 107th Avenue, Miami, FL 33174   305-559-6715

HAWAII
1143 Bishop Street, Honolulu, HI 96813   808-521-2731

ILLINOIS
172 North Michigan Avenue, Chicago, IL 60601   312-346-4228

LOUISIANA
4403 Veterans Memorial Blvd, Metairie, LA 70006   504-887-7631

MASSACHUSETTS
885 Providence Hwy, Dedham, MA 02026   781-326-5385

MISSOURI
9804 Watson Road, St. Louis, MO 63126   314-965-3512

NEW YORK
115 E. 29th Street, New York City, NY 10016   212-754-1110

SOUTH CAROLINA
243 King Street, Charleston, SC 29401   843-577-0175

TEXAS
No book center; for parish exhibits or outreach evangelization, contact: 210-569-0500, or SanAntonio@paulinemedia.com, or P.O. Box 761416, San Antonio, TX 78245

VIRGINIA
1025 King Street, Alexandria, VA 22314   703-549-3806

CANADA
3022 Dufferin Street, Toronto, ON M6B 3T5   416-781-9131